Cowboy Poetry Matters

Cowboy Poetry Matters
From Abilene to the Mainstream

CONTEMPORARY COWBOY WRITING

Edited and with an Introduction
by Robert McDowell

Story Line Press
2000

Published by Story Line Press, Three Oaks Farm, PO Box 1240, Ashland, OR 97520-0055
www.storylinepress.com

This publication was made possible thanks in part to the generous support of the National Endowment for the Arts, the Nicholas Roerich Museum, the San Francisco Foundation, the Charles Schwab Foundation, the Oregon Arts Commission, and our individual contributors.

The editor wishes to thank Linda Hussa and Paul Zarzyski without whose generous guidance and help this book would not have been possible.

Book design by Lysa McDowell
Cover oil painting by Teresa Schleigh

Library of Congress Cataloging-in-Publication Data Pending

Cowboy poetry matters : from Abilene to the mainstream : contemporary cowboy writing / edited by Robert McDowell.
    p. cm.
    ISBN 1-885266-89-8 (alk. paper)
1. Cowboys—Poetry. 2. Ranch life—Poetry. 3. American poetry,West (U.S.) 4. American poetry—20th century. 5. West (U.S.)—Poetry. I. McDowell, Robert, 1953–

PS595.C6 C7 2000
811.008'092636—dc21   99-089819

ACKNOWLEDGMENTS

J. B. Allen's poems appear by permission of the author and Grey Horse Press (1997); Virginia Bennett's poems appear courtesy of the author; Jon Bowerman's poems are published here by permission of the author; Robert R. Brown's poems are published here by permission of the author; Laurie Wagner Buyer's "When I Came West," "Madge," and "Smell of Sage" are reprinted from her volume, *Glass-eyed Paint in the Rain* (1996), with permission of the author and High Plains Press; "Bareback," "Letters," and "Kneading Bread," are reprinted from *Red Colt Canyon*; the poems of John C. Dofflemyer appear with the permission of the author; Dana Gioia's essay appears courtesy of the author and Graywolf Press; Tami Haaland's poems are reprinted here courtesy of the author; Donald Hall's "Names of Horses" appears here with the permission of the author, as well as the publisher of the volume, *Old and New Poems*, Ticknor & Fields; "Beef Eater," "Butchering the Crippled Heifer," "What the Falcon Said," and "Coffee Cup Café" by Linda M. Hasselstrom appear from the volume, *Land Circle, Writings Collected from the Land*, with the permission of Fulcrum Publishing. "Haying: A Four-Part Definition," "Hands," and "My Last Will and Testament" appear with the permission of the author; Linda Hussa's poems, "Give Us Rain!", "Swans," "The Man Shoeing a Horse and His Little Girl," "Playing at Doctor," and "In the Evening Autumn," appear here courtesy of the author and The Black Rock Press. The poems, "I Fix the Fence—the Fence Fixes Me," "Dear Child," and "Love Letters," are reprinted with the permission of the author and Gibbs Smith, Publisher. "Dewclaw" is published with the permission of the author; Tony Johnston's poems appear courtesy of the author; Maxine Kumin's poems are reprinted with permission of the author and W. W. Norton and Company; Linda McCarriston's poems first appeared in the following magazines: "Le Coursier de Jeanne D'Arc" in *The Georgia Review*, "A Thousand Genuflections" (which won the Consuelo Ford Award from the Poetry Society of America) in *Triquarterly*, "Riding Out at Evening," "On Horseback," and "Bucked" in *Poetry*, and "With the Horse in the Winter Pasture" in *The Ohio Review*. We thank the author, and the editors and publishers of these magazines, for permission to include the poems here; Nancy McLelland's essay is published with the permission of the author; Wallace McRae's "Two Mountain Stones: Cowboy Character Studies" is reprinted with the permission of the author. The poems, with his permission and that of Gibbs Smith, Publisher, are reprinted from the collection, *Cowboy Curmudgeon and Other Poems*; Joel Nelson's poems are reprinted here with the permission of the author; Kathy Ogren's essay is published with the permission of the author; Thelma Poirier's poems appear courtesy of the author; Buck Ramsey's poems appear here with the generous permission of Mrs. Buck (Bette) Ramsey; "My Pony," from the volume, *American Prodigal*, by Liam Rector, is reprinted with the permission of the author and Story Line Press; Andy Wilkinson's poems appear courtesy of the author; Paul Zarzyski's poems and essay appear with the kind permission of the author. His poems, "Buck," "All This Way for the Short Ride," "To Wallace," and "Hip-Cocked Broncs," are also reprinted, courtesy of Museum of New Mexico Press, from his collection, *All This Way for the Short Ride: Roughstock Sonnets 1971-1996*. His essay, *The Lariati Versus/Verses the Literati: Loping Toward Dana Gioia's Dream Come Real*, is reprinted from the anthology, *Writing Montana: Literature Under the Big Sky*, edited by Rick Newby and Suzanne Hunger, Montana Center for the Book, 1996.

TABLE OF CONTENTS

POETRY

POETRY

POETRY

POETRY IN MEMOIR

ESSAYS

CONTRIBUTORS NOTES

COWBOY POETRY ANTHOLOGIES OF NOTE

For Dylan, Eoghan, and Jane

&

For cowboys and cowgirls at heart everywhere

COWBOY POETRY—OF THE HEART, OF THE MIND

INTRODUCTION BY ROBERT MCDOWELL

What do you think of when you hear the term, *Cowboy poetry*? When I was a boy in the 1950s, I'm certain that Cowboy poetry would have been synonymous, in my mind, with singing cowboys. That meant Gene Autry, Roy Rogers, Tex Ritter, and many others. Though I see now that the comparison was not altogether inaccurate, it left a lot out of the true picture. But just what does that look like?

If you polled a dozen strangers (just for fun, I did this at a Burger King off exit 33 in Medford, Oregon—a fast food joint featuring a beautiful bust of Tom Mix amidst impressive western decor, and old poetry festival posters on the bathroom walls), you're likely to get a dozen answers. The responses I gathered on that occasion included: "I have no idea"; "Baxter Black" (the veterinarian-turned-poet who can often be heard on national radio); "Elko, Nevada" (site of the largest annual Cowboy poetry festival); "You know, rhymed, funny stuff"; "Garth Brooks"; "the late Marty Robbins, *El Paso* trilogy"; and, my favorite, "Stuff guys do when they should be out workin'." All of these responses—except, perhaps, the last one—make some sense. But a lot of what Cowboy poetry *is* is missing from all of them.

The purpose of this anthology is to round up the cattle after the stampede, to restore order from the dust and chaos, and thereby provide this missing matter. The poems, essays, and creative nonfiction gathered here demonstrate and explore Cowboy poetry's essential and important place in our literary mainstream. Hence the appropriate inclusion of poets like Donald Hall, Maxine Kumin, and Liam Rector, as well as Dana Gioia's controversial essay, *Can Poetry Matter?* Our goal is to treat Cowboy poetry, and writing about Cowboy poetry, with the seriousness it deserves. It is also to recognize and display the explosion of important writing by western women over the last fifteen years. Also, in this age of contemporary literature classes and writing workshops, we hope that this anthology assists teachers in bringing an essential contribution to our serious literature into classrooms everywhere.

❋ ❋ ❋

On some important level, the night guard singing to cattle shares a bond with mainstream poets reading on the contemporary circuit. Whether the

poet reads from the Elko stage to five thousand, or from the campus plat-
form to fifty, recitation, with its formal necessities, is very much at the
heart of the poetry. Nancy McLelland in her essay explores the orality of
Cowboy poetry, placing it within the Bardic, Homeric tradition, while
Dana Gioia calls our attention to the very successful ways that Cowboy
poetry uses the same outlets as popular entertainment to reach larger
audiences than mainstream poetry, secure in the academy, has been able
to muster. Forming the bedrock of the prose and poetry collected here
are recurrent themes of apprenticeship, inheritance, learning-by-doing,
the outcast bearing witness to a life that is both at the core of our national
identity, and at the same time, long gone in the experience of the vast
majority.

How could the cowboy life, if it were to endure, become anything but a
myth, a sprawling legend? How can some part of us fail to be seduced by
it? Doesn't every person see the loner in himself, the adventurer in her-
self? Denying it is to deny a necessary truth about our American selves.

Many arguments debunking this western vision point to the relatively
brief historical period when the range was truly open, the cowboy genu-
inely free. Often, the aim of such arguments is to call into question the truth-
fulness of western writers, to suggest that the lives they are writing about
have as much honest currency in them as western life in the movies.

It is useful, when questioning those who express such views, to note
how little they have read around in the work they criticize. Professional
commentators stereotype writers they have not read, then pass their pro-
nouncements on to readers as fact. This is how the criticism of dismissal,
despite its significant ironies, steams along. Isn't it odd that many main-
stream critics deplore the poetry and prose of contemporary ranch and
rodeo life in an age when the banal confession has been so celebrated in
literature? Could this be a reactionary response to a way of life one does
not immediately understand or identify with? Could it be snobbery, or
something more complicated, such as publicly loathing what one privately
admires? Most of us have lived all our lives in cities and towns, maintain-
ing at best a tenuous, cinematic connection to cowboy culture. Some of us
experienced Sunday visits to relatives living on small farms or ranches. But
as we grew older, encouraged to pack away our visions of western life with
other childish things, weren't we also pressured to accept the citified, grown-
up view that our rural kin were failures who missed out by clinging to a life of
the past? It seems likely that something very near this attitude has worked
against Cowboy poetry's acceptance in the mainstream.

❄ ❄ ❄

The cowboy life is very much an occupation, a livelihood to many women and men, and to most of the contributors to this book. But it is also, perhaps most compellingly so, a state of mind.

It has a lot to do with proximity to animals. Numbingly urban and sophisticated, how often do we forget our spiritual and physiological connections to the land and to animals? How often do we deny them? We do many things that are not good for us; forgetting and denial are among them. If we pay attention, living among animals makes us more aware of our own rhythms. The cat and dog only mirror us, but the deliberate patterns and long memory of the horse make it possible for us to feel more deeply the changing of seasons, the turning of the earth. It makes one realize how willful, frenetic, and self-destructive our modern town life can be. And yet, it is so hard to turn from it, to throw off its shrouds. Mucking out a stall, taking a turn in the arena, or turning horses out in a big field and watching them communicate with one another is to miss the pastoral tradition (brilliantly explored in Kathy Ogren's essay); it is to feel a certain longing for that far away moment in time when we turned to embrace modern progress, which made us sorry in ways that most of us could not have anticipated.

An active life among animals revives the natural being in us. It restores perspective, sensation, belief. Cowboy poetry and cowboy writing, rooted in folkore, legends, and the life of the land, accept this as fundamental truth.

※ ※ ※

The poetry that endures is always regional in its character and personality. Robert Frost, tempered by his California roots, imbued New England stoicism with a far west sense of anxiety and adventure. Marianne Moore's verses, at their best, evoke Brooklyn and New York. Robinson Jeffers wrote memorable lyrics and sweeping epics that could not exist without their grasp of history and their settings on the haunting, dramatic Big Sur coast. Robert Penn Warren's poetry is impossible to imagine without its Southern anchor. Emily Dickinson's majestic, fragile poems of passion and brilliance mirror the cultural center that was Amherst in the late nineteenth century.

Poetry essentially offers its readers an often overlooked attraction, the ability *to go* there, which is to say *elsewhere*, a place that one would like to visit or know better. At the same time, poetry gives its author the chance to play the role of proud or reproachful tour guide, to entertain, amuse, or instruct while leading us through a private place.

The best Cowboy poetry also stays home, taking shape in a compelling landscape that is inhabited by unique animals and people. Like all good poetry, it knows its own weather, its own topography, and through its keen sense of family history, it has inspired new notions of community.

This last point may, at first, seem confusing to some given the fact that the original practitioners were adventurers who in coming west left their families far behind. But nothing serves so well as loss to cast some person, or some thing, you need in high relief. Far from family and community, it could not have been long before the original cowboys and cowgirls felt, perhaps more deeply than they ever had, the importance of such connections. At that point, they banded together to survive, later to work. Eventually, they created new families and new communities. Having lost or given up on these institutions once, they formed new alliances with perhaps a deeper sense of commitment, which embodied a pioneering sense of responsibility to tradition, to friends and neighbors, to communal labor itself. Cowboy poetry embraces the same values.

Finally, I suspect that the current flowering of Cowboy poetry has something to do with the revival of religious poetry in America. "America may be God-crazy," the prize-winning poet, Charles Simic, declared in a 1998 citation in *The Nation* honoring Mark Jarman's *Questions for Ecclesiastes*, and at the end of this millennium, surely he was right. Simic also pointed out that ever since Emerson, American poets have had only the absence of God to ponder. It would be less than wise to claim that Cowboy poetry ignores Emerson, that it sidesteps doubt, but surely it shrinks that Sage's significance.

Doubt, when it exists in most cowboy poems, is concerned with unpredictable weather, the deep mysteries of animals, the sum total of one's earthly deeds and the eternal reward, or punishment, that will surely be meted out—the very inscrutability of the Supreme Being. If we agree, in fact, that in Cowboy poetry God is unquestionably present, that the image of God is held in the mind and heart with great confidence, then we may be able to agree after all on this poetry's popularity, especially among its many nonacademic readers. Perhaps we can say that Cowboy poetry approaches, with considerable respect, the spiritual questions that we have raised, and whose answers we've pursued, under loose reins here on earth.

POETRY

WISPS

He sits by a battered old table
That rivals his three-score-and-ten,
Its surface worn smooth by the cups and the plates
And the coats of forgotten old men.

The fire casts its light 'cross the craigs of his face
And fights for its space on the wall
Where shadows are dancin' with mem'ries
To the tune of the night herder's call.

The wind draws the specters of happier times
Through cracks in the weathered old door
While coffee grows cold in the lone rusty cup
And mice play their games on the floor.

Unconsciously easin' the pain in his hip
From broncs better fed to a dog,
A smile wipes the frown from the depths of his eyes
And scatters the withering fog.

Indelible choices dictated the trails
Whose endings were known in advance,
Fer youngsters absorbed by the smoke and the dust
Never linger to finish the dance.

Resigned to the fate fortune dealt to the game
He rises to welcome the sun,
Another day started in silence alone
Forgettin' what might have been done.

Old Time don't diminish the crux of a choice
Though circumstance may cloud the view,
Fer things that we wish might have been or could be
Seldom travel with things that we do.

NIGHTHAWK NOTIONS

When the last big calf runs bawlin' to his anxious mama's side,
Trailin' wisps of smoke still curlin' from his hair,
You find yourself a wishin' there was one more bunch to brand
'Fore ol' Cousie turns the wagon t'wards his lair.

He claims to like a stove and roof to ply his skillful trade
And there's times when he's convinced that it's the truth.
But I notice when the shoein' starts his eyes begin to gleam
Like the sunlight off that one gold-plated tooth.

The crippled leg that put an end to helpin' make the drives
Didn't kill the cowboy livin' deep inside
And his grouchy disposition more'n likely mirrors rage
At the twist of fate that signaled his last ride.

Ol' Slim says he 'uz a good 'un 'fore the fall that laid 'im up,
Took to drinkin' purty bad, the story goes,
Till the boss went in and dragged 'im from the Drover's Rest Saloon—
Figgered he was worth the trouble, I suppose.

That was way before my time, but I've been wonder'n' here of late
If there maybe ain't some kin between them two,
Though it's always strictly bizness 'round the shack or wagon fly,
Never visitin' 'til the workin's fin'lly through.

Anyhow, it's good to see 'im with that banty rooster strut,
Rulin' punchers, camp, and wagon like a king.
Maybe all the cows, come brandin' time, has had themselves some twins—
Takin' twice as long to do the work next spring.

THE MEDICINE KEEPERS

A man might live and work beside
The fellers 'round the wagon
And never say two words unless
It's just hooraw and braggin'.

But sometimes in the solitude
Of some ol' line camp shack
He smooths a fruit can label out
And writes there on its back

A group of words redeemed from time
To last when he moves on,
Set down with hurried flourish
'Fore his mem'ry of 'em's gone.

The spellin' may not be exact
Or commas where they ought,
But there within those rugged lines
A mood is somehow caught.

It might be full of sadness
From a death or crippled friend,
To just the mournful yearnin'
For a way that's bound to end.

Some others could be bawdy
While full of life and mirth
Or stories 'bout some saddle horse
That has no peers on earth.

There's many through the years been lost
Or burned or throwed away,
But others yet survive
To give us views of yesterday.

And still amongst the workin' hands
The words come now and then
To write a livin' history
Of the stock, and earth, and men.

TREASURES

Do you mind some cold, clear mornin' settin' horseback on a bluff
When the air was still and ringin' in yore ears,
And you orta been a-foggin' down amongst the rocks and brush
To make it to that gunyun 'fore them steers?

There was sumpthin' sorta held you in that frozen speck of time,
Paintin' pictures for the mem'ry times a-comin',
Till you leaned up on them swells and put that bronc down off the edge
And heard that weathered hat brim go to hummin'.

Things were boomin' back at home while you was pullin' second guard,
Accordin' to the letter that was brought,
But the sudden thought of leavin' was a thing just too blame hard
When a feller had what wizards dearly sought.

Lanky yearlin' colts a-dancin' as the mares slipped in to drink
While you used them stunted cedars for a blind,
Takin' notice of a grulla runnin' circles 'round the rest—
And you aimed to keep that hombre on yore mind.

Or them new calves just a bouncin' on that early springtime grass
As the sun was turnin' hair to shinin' silk,
While them high-horned baby sitters kept a watchful, wary eye
On a country from the Pecos to the Milk.

Winter dances, and the widder—mighty lithesome, warm, and sweet—
Always makin' shore each cowboy got a dance
Though she made 'em mind their manners and 'twas plain, without a doubt,
That young banker claimed the last 'un in advance.

Them's the things that fill yore innards for the hard times up ahead
When yore plunder and yore bankroll's come apart,
All them weeks of steady drizzle or the dust from ridin' drag
Just a-peelin' off the bark to show the heart.

REASONS FOR STAYIN'

"What's the myst'ry of the wagon?" asked a towny, green as grass,
As he vis'ted on a dreary autumn day
Fer there weren't a sign of romance nor no waddies 'round with class,
And he couldn't see why one would want to stay.

"Well, don't be askin' me," says Jake, when asked that very thing,
"I've only been around here thirty years;
If I'd learnt some floocy answers to the questions you-all bring
I'd not be tough as brushy outlawed steers!

"It's a dang sight more romantic in the bunkhouse, snug and warm,
When that winter wind is blowin' from the Pole
Than the livin' at the wagon through the same ol' freezin' storm
And the call of nature sends you for a stroll!

"The smell of beans and beefsteak born on bilin' coffee's breath
Pulls a feller from them soogans, clean and dry,
'Stead of half-cooked food that's drown'ded so you'll not git choked to death
As you look around and git to wonderin' why.

"But, I reckon, since you asked me, it's the challenge that you git
Testin' what you got for gizzard through the squalls,
And not just nature's doin's, but the kind that's stirred a bit
When a cowboy, bronc, or critter starts the brawls.

"Take them fellers that's a-squattin' 'round that soggy campfire there,
That big-un's done some time for murder one,
But I'll guarantee you, feller, when you think your flank is bare
You'll hear his boomin' laughter through the run.

"That scroungy-lookin' half-breed kid can ride a bear or lion,
Though he mostly rides the rough-uns for the boys.
Black Pete would rope the Devil through a stand of burnt-out pine,
And Ol' Dobb would mark his ears to hear the noise!

"What I'm gittin' 'round to sayin' is them boys will back yore play
Though their outside shore ain't groomed or show-ring slick;
It's their innards that you count on when you work for puncher's pay,
And the reason why the wagon makes you stick."

THE LION

She waits in the deep, dense forest
Lurking in the shadows where the sun is defied
Lapping water from an ice-encrusted stream
She is stealth wrapped up in a tawny hide.

She hears more by instinct than by listening
Her paws like radar upon the glistening shale
And, she's keenly aware, when you are two miles away,
Of your horse as he plods up the trail.

She has ample time to consider her options
Whether scientists believe she can reason or not.
She could stay where she's at, undetected,
Or head back up the slope at a trot.

Instead, she crosses your path when you're almost upon her,
Like a dancing sunbeam teasing a child.
Leaving her track in the trail just to inform you . . .
You've been that close to something that wild.

SOCIAL JUSTICE

In an orange grove outside of Phoenix
An artificial forest where pesticides dwell,
Migrant workers pick hard-luck dreams.
Hot, sweaty days spent in a hazy Hell.

Forty-five men in a clapboard shanty
Share one couch, one bed, one chair.
Where perfect teeth flash weary smiles
From faces creased from life unfair.

All of them share one ladle.
Tortillas are dishes for forty-five men.
Here, breakfast, lunch and late-night supper
Will be a burrito . . . a burrito . . . and . . . yet again.

Hopes hang like Christmas ornaments.
Citrus orbs bring pennies a fifty-pound bag.
Funding dreams of reunited family
Underneath a striped and starry flag.

Sadly marred and battle-scarred,
With ladder-bruised shoulders, they meet
In a yard where no bugs or birds dare to live,
Their only escape from the harvest-time heat.

Thirty thousand feet above their highest rungs,
A 757 heads for Miami from L.A.
And a woman lets the whole plane know that
She's damned upset with her seat assignment today.

TAPESTRY OF KNOTS

In the quiet-time of morning,
    when the moon is going down,
She builds a cookstove fire
    with yester-news from town.
And, as warmth creeps into the cabin,
    measured slowly by degrees,
She sits with pen at kitchen table
    with a quilt to warm her knees.

And she writes of thoughts she garnered
    during chores of day before
While she pitched the hay from feed sled
    which she prayed would travel slower.
Upon her pad of yellow paper
    dormant words came into life,
Her mind crept beyond the mundane walls,
    before she became a rancher's wife.

She could travel (at the speed of ink)
    to those places in the heart
When romance bloomed like summer's rose
    or a dream broke and fell apart.
She still could see, with clarity,
    a dozen years gone past,
When love was new or love was cold
    or a spirit had been slashed.

With open, honest invitation
    to explore her hidden thoughts,
She scribed haunting, hunted images
    like a tapestry of knots.
And she typed them up on linen paper
    so they'd be worthy to be read
Then, she donned her crusted coveralls
    for there were cattle to be fed.

How many more are like her?
   We can only guess.
The women who write heart-broke words,
   emboldened to confess.
They fold, they stamp, and they mail
   their souls from coast to coast
And share their work with all the world
   except the one they love the most.

SUCH CONTROL

With just one movement of the hands
One mindless lifting on the sash
Across the peeling windowsill
The world rushes in, in a flash.

        The evening killdeer cry their fears,
        The nightbirds croon their evening tune.
        A flirty mare greets wished-for lovers,
        While, far-off, a coyote courts the moon.

A lonesome calf calls for its mother
A burdened branch creaks beneath its load
And a half-mile distant, a semi-truck
Shifts gears to travel the rambling road.

        Arriving like an unwelcome guest,
        A scented, wanton wind drifts in.
        Her heady perfume hypnotizes . . .
        Alluring hints of where she's been.

A waft of frozen mountain meadows,
A touch of sagebrush on the hill.
Infant cheatgrass, re-emerging
All march across the windowsill.

        They toy with curtains, set them dancing
        Have their way with skittish papers
        The way they act, you can be sure
        They've not been disciplined for their capers.

They next travel up and down the spine
Now it's time to turn this thing about
And, with just one movement of the hands . . .
The sash is closed . . . and the world is locked out.

CALVIN'

This neighbor of mine got hisself in a bind
Workin' on a calvy young cow
Kinda crowded his luck when he found her calf stuck
And was darn near adopted . . . by the cow.

Now that heifer was down, stretched out on the ground,
The labor pains they were intense.
An impending disaster out there in the pasture,
Long ways from a tree or a fence.

There was nothing to tie to so he figured he'd try to
Pull the calf where she lay in the dirt
He got the chains ready and held the cow steady
While he rolled up the sleeves of his shirt.

One foot was in sight so he figured he might
Get the chain fastened on if he tried.
But before it was on, the foot was withdrawn
And he had to reach way down inside.

He got one loop on, right where it belonged
And worked 'til he got it snubbed tight.
The feelin' around he finally found
The other foot bent back to the right.

The contractions were coming with such force it was numbing.
The calf's tongue was startin' to swell.
His arm cramped so intense that he thought it made sense
To let the cow rest for a spell.

But it seems that she knew, 'cause before he withdrew
His arm from its cramped up condition
She suddenly leaped up onto her feet
And put him in a per'lous position.

One loop on the calf, the other 'bout half
Fastened around on his hand
She jerked out the slack when she came untracked
And that's where this story really began . . .

Jerked from his knees, the chain wouldn't release
So he's bangin' along through the rocks.
Then she turned with a rush out through the sage
and a breaker in the pen.

He dug in his toes, but ya' know how it goes,
He hadn't a ghost of a chance
To slow the cow down, she just kept foggin' on
'Til she drug him half out of his pants.

When she quit runnin' at last he lay there aghast . . .
The cow was lickin' him off and implied
Don't lay there cursin' get up an' start nursin'
'Fore I lick all the hair off your hide.

There's a moral of course. Use a tractor or horse
When you can't get your cow in the chute.
You may pull her in two but whatever you do
You won't lose your pants and your boots.

THE SATURDAY MATINEE

I still recall that early day
When we went to the Saturday matinee
There was Roy and Hoppy and Lash LaRue
Gene Autry and a lot of others too.
They rode good horses and they all packed guns
But it seems they never killed anyone.
They never ran from a stand up fight
But they always fought fair and did what was right.
When threatened by a rustler band
They shot the guns from the outlaws' hands.
They had truth and honor and all the traits
That makes a hero really great.
And after the Saturday matinee
When we all went outside to play
We lived by the "The Code" and could understand
Only shoot at the guns in the bad guys' hands
Back when playin' cowboys was all in fun
And real heroes never killed anyone.

LAST VISIT WITH THE BANKER

Sittin' there in the Beggar's Chair
In the banker's office that day
He talked about the effects of the drought
And whether cows could eat hay.

You said they would, and really should . . .
"But the question is can you afford,"
He says, "to pay the interest each day
To cover their room and board?

"Now the rates had went to eighteen percent
When you bought that set of cattle
But we underwrote and you signed the note
With your house and your soul as collateral.

"Now you say you need feed and bulls to breed
Those cows that the bank still owns.
Why do you come around when the rates are down
To try and renew your loan?"

Then his face got red, but he smiled as he said,
"I'm callin' your note today,
'Cuz calves have went to fifty cents
And you can't afford to feed 'em hay.

"But I won't take your house. An' you can keep your spouse
And those cows and calves as well.
But set your lid and grease your skids . . .
I'm gonna have your soul in Hell!"

Well friend, don't fret, it ain't over yet.
The Lord has provided a way.
When the future looks dim, just call on Him
You won't see that banker on judgement day.

THE HUNTER

I've come here to the county court
To ask you Judge for your support
I was going hunting yesterday
And found a gate, locked, in my way!
Now private property be damned!
I don't request but do demand
The lock be cut and thrown away
And that gate removed from in my way.

And I suggest that you don't hesitate
To resolve this problem of the gate,
But do exactly as I say.
Or I'll go out and find a way
Not only to have the gate removed
But you, your Honor as well; I'll prove
That you're as worthless as can be
If you don't respond immediately.

I'll drive down the barrow ditch
And carry a bar and shovel with which
I'll pry the gate posts from the ground
And hide them where they can't be found,
And travel anywhere I please
And loot and shoot and cut down trees.
'Cuz the license that I bought to hunt
I consider a permit to do just what I want.

THE RUNAWAYS

We'd only been married a week or two
When I got Belle and Caesar and some harness too.
My wife looked 'em over from the corner of her eye
But she never said a word or asked me why
If I had so darned much work to do
I could do it with horses . . . especially those two!

It wasn't that they were on the fight
But both their eyes showed a lot of white.
You might be able to call 'em a pair,
Not a team, but they'd get you there.
Belle was a Belgian, short and stout,
Pull 'til you'd think your arms'd give out.

She'd been a loggin' horse in the woods,
Snap those tugs to start, she would.
Caesar was a Percheron, long and lean,
Eighteen hands and more it seemed.
He was really just a big old colt
But when Belle hit the collar, Caesar'd bolt.

Long legged Caesar, he'd jump right out,
Get a half a length lead or thereabout,
Then Belle had to catch up or she knew she'd feel
The single tree bangin' her on the heel,
Then I tell ya' the race was on
Don't be lookin' around 'cause they'd be gone.

I hitched 'em to a pasture harrow 12 foot wide
And holdin' the lines well out to the side
Took up the slack but then somehow
They took up more, and more, AND HOW!
I would't say they ever really hit their stride,
More like shot from a cannon or tryin' to fly.

There might have been a spot or two where that harrow touched
But it didn't slow 'em down 'cause it didn't touch much.
It's probably a good thing I had long lines
So when they jerked me down I could drag behind.
The snaps on my shirt were gettin' hot
The cow pies were soft but the rocks were not.

When they turned the corner I was holdin' tight
Then they hooked the fence and I lost the fight.
Turned loose of those lines as fence posts cracked,
Belle and Caesar never even looked back,
Just shifted up to a higher gear
Like somethin' was catchin' up from the rear.

They were draggin' posts and wire beside —
Now that harrow looked forty feet wide
But it was dang sure breakin' up the crust,
Cow pies exploded in a cloud of dust.
At the other end of the field that harrow got caught
In some trees and tugs broke like a rifle shot.

But Belle and Caesar just thundered on
'Til they finally got tired and came back to the barn
My wife had 'em just about put away
When I limped into the house that day
My clothes were dirty and stained and torn,
Why I only had half of the shirt I'd worn.

Her face was kinda pale and white
'Course she'd seen it all and musta' been a sight.
But she gave me one of those kind of looks
That tells ya' more than if she'd wrote a book,
Then finally looked me square in the eye,
And shakin' a little like she might cry,

Says "If they were bound and determined to have it so,
Why didn't you just let 'em go?"
Well, I didn't have an answer that made much sense
Though I was tryin' to keep 'em out of that fence
But I says, "Honey I had all I could do
To hold on to those lines . . . I couldn't let go, too!"

MYSTERIOUS MAIDEN

In the Superstition Mountains,
Where the Dutchman's mine is lost,
And the twisted trails and canyons,
Make the gold not worth the cost.

There's a maiden dressed in buckskin,
Who is seen by very few,
But she leaves a burning question,
In the minds of those who do.

For she leads a painted pony,
With an old man on its back,
Whose sightless eyes keep staring,
At a world that's always black.

The rattlesnakes don't rattle,
As the two go drifting by,
Though the buzzards all come wheeling,
To that lonesome stretch of sky.

If you ever ride those mountains,
Then perhaps one day you'll meet,
That pretty dark-haired maiden,
With the buckskin on her feet.

But she'll leave no tracks behind her,
As she rounds the nearest bend,
And the only sound you'll hear,
Is the sighing of the wind.

And if you round the bend behind her,
You will stop and stare in awe,
As the empty trail before you,
Makes you wonder what you saw.

Other cowboys that you meet there,
Say they never saw the pair,
Of the blind man and the maiden,
With the long black braided hair,

Your searching eyes will tell you,
What your mind already knows,
That they're nowhere on that trail,
And there's no place they could go.

Though the sun is shining brightly,
You will shiver from the cold,
And the memory will haunt you,
Through the years as you grow old.

OLD NEVER

Bill Hogan jammed his hat down,
Then nodded at the gate.
He knew the next eight seconds,
Were in the hands of fate.

The bull was called Old Never,
Cause he never had been rode,
And when that gate swung open,
Old Never would explode.

Bill felt the muscles gather,
As Old Never planned ahead.
And a fleeting thought went through him,
Of some cowboys left for dead.

The crowd sat hushed in silence,
As the gate swung open wide.
The time for thinking over,
Nothing left to do but ride.

Then the sunshine seemed to darken,
And he lost all sense of sound,
As Old Never changed direction,
While five feet off the ground.

The dust began to billow,
And Bill's nose began to bleed,
But he kept his balance somehow,
As he rode that evil breed.

His eyes were out of focus,
And his teeth were jarring loose.
All the years of his experience,
Were of very little use.

As that ride went on forever,
He began to wonder why,
He hadn't picked a faster,
And more easy way to die.

Then faintly in the distance,
He heard a whistle blow,
But his addled brain forgot to tell,
His left hand to let go.

And Old Never wasn't finished,
Cause he didn't know the rules.
His one and only purpose,
Was the bucking off of fools.

The clowns were acting cautious,
Cause each horn was two feet long,
And the seconds seemed like hours,
As he kept on hanging on.

But at last the message got there,
And his fingers they went slack.
And he was quickly catapulted,
Up and off Old Never's back.

And he landed with a jarring thud,
On that hard arena floor,
Where Old Never tried to gore him,
Just to even up the score.

Bill's thoughts were a little fuzzy,
And not making too much sense.
Thank goodness someone grabbed him,
And helped him climb the fence,

And later on some cowboy said,
They should change Old Never's name,
Bill Hogan stood right up and said,
"No. Leave the name the same.

Maybe, just this one time,
He let a cowboy win,
But this is one tough old bull rider,
Who'll never ride that bull again."

CHARLIE JONES

Ol' Charlie Jones shoed horses,
And possessed uncommon skill,
At taking wild-eyed ponies,
And making them stand still.

They wouldn't move a muscle,
Or so it has been said,
While he pumped upon the bellows,
Until that forge was gleaming red.

Then trimmed away at every hoof,
And hammered on each shoe.
You knew the job was perfect,
When Ol' Charlie Jones was through.

He'd walk without a tremor,
Up to nervous young mustangs,
And have them standing quiet,
While that nine-pound hammer rang.

Cowboys came from miles around,
To watch him do his thing,
And often they brought with them,
The roughest of their string.

But Charlie handled every one,
As though it were a pet.
If there's a horse too tough for him,
They haven't found it yet.

So Charlie's reputation grew,
And men were heard to brag,
That only Charlie Jones,
Could put a shoe on their old nag.

Ranchers came a riding in,
And offered him good pay,
To come on out and shoe their herd,
A short-day's ride away.

But Charlie wouldn't budge from town,
No matter what they tried,
Cause, one thing that they never knew,
Charlie was afraid to ride.

WHEN I CAME WEST

When I came west
I had never seen an elk, autumn dun
and bright buff, or heard an errant
owl ghost call from the thick shadow
of a pine, smelled the sharp tang
of wood smoke wreathed in my hair
or washed half naked in the glacial
spill rush of a river half a world away.

I never knew the gut deep intimate
warmth of milking goats, scattering
wheat for squabbling hens, the uncommon
joy of breaking bales for frost-crusted
horses, the mystery of unraveling a tale
of tracks and blood in the snow,
the silk-sand tongue of a cat washing
my stub-nailed and milk-stained hands.

In the remote rootcellar's dank
darkness, fear crawled over my skin,
dim candle light flickering over
thousands of hibernating daddy-longlegs
that clutched the ceiling in spidered clusters
as I knelt to rub away sandy soil from
strange roots—rutabaga, turnip, beet—
scrubbed them one by one on the riverbank.

Obscure spring soil gave up her bounty
of earthworms shoveled from their subterranean
sleep. Kissed by the newly awakened power
of the sun, I watched them writhe and weave
back into black earth where I planted
rows of peas and beans, coaxed strawberries
out of winter's wrap of mulch and straw,
rinsed my hands in a snow melt pond.

Loneliness lurked in my heart's smallest
corner. Once an enemy kept carefully
at bay by city lights I called her out face
to face everyday, tasted her name on my
silent tongue, turned her into an uncanny
comfort, wrapped her around me like fur,
danced with the dog, sang under the stars,
rode wild on a glass-eyed paint in the rain.

MADGE

They say she whacked off her hair
and crammed on a hat,
dressed like a man,
cussed and chewed,
married her hired hands
so she wouldn't have to
pay 'em any wages,
told 'em if they wanted
smokes and booze
to get off their butts
and trap for cash.

When they left, fed up,
she just married another,
outliving them all
until she dropped dead
of a heart attack
in front of the old wood range
while building biscuits.

Forty years later
I still felt her essence
coming down the stairs
into the cold kitchen;
I'd light the lamp quickly
and save the single match
to fire up paper and kindling
carefully set in the stove.

"Move over, Madge," I'd whisper,
"Gonna have pancakes today."

At night her old homestead
house creaked and groaned,
keeping company with the wild
roar of the wide glacial river.

Every spring her crocus
and narcissus bloomed bright
below the south-face windows.

So far from town, no one
close enough to call or visit,
I found myself talking
to her when I was alone:

"Keep the fire goin' Madge,
I'm gonna shovel snow."

SMELL OF SAGE

Autumns ago, we rode bareback for sage,
crossing and re-crossing river channels,
urging our mounts through ancient sloughs,
brush-choked islands. We talked then,
sometimes sang, passing the miles with
laughter until reaching the vista:

Sage creek poured out of Canada,
long bars of pebbled sand, and above,
a bluff so high we craned our necks
to see a wizened pine on top. The horses
tugged their bits, wanting to run;
we whooped and shouted, plunged cross
the creek mouth and down smooth bars;
sun and spray dazzling our eyes until
the horses lost all footing and swam,
wide-eyed and snorting for the bank.

The lone pine wore our dripping clothes,
your buckskins and moccasins, my socks and jeans —
the clash of cultures hanging in a tree — still,
stringing us together, our vision of mated
redtails circling the sky and the drifting
smell of sage.

Toweled by wind, we descended, the horses
haunch-sliding their way down rocky deer
trails. The flat was endless; a prehistoric
riverbed, aspen ringed, where now sagebrush grew.
Leaving the horses to trail their reins, we knelt,
snipped silver-green leaves into a leather pouch,
the herb to spice our sausage and stew, the pungent
odor filling our afternoon.

This autumn, returning to your world, I thought
that time lost to us. But, mid-winter, unknowing,
a visiting friend brought with her a sprig of sage.
By lamplight, watching you stitch a deer skin, she
unbraided and brushed my tangled hair. The smell
of sage reached us, seeping through our differences,
tying a loose, but lasting, common bond.

BAREBACK

Seeping through dusty jeans
his heat thaws my thighs
loosens chilled stiffness from my spine

and my shoulders relax, breasts bounce,
clench muscles grip his heaving sides
as we lope circles in dusky sage.

Hoof beats pound through my pelvis
uniting hips and hocks —
his heart throbs with mine

as we shift our center of balance
switch leads on the fly,
nostrils flared, sweating,

we cut the last of the day
from October's long-edged night.

LETTERS

All her life she lived remote on ranches,
far from folks and goings on
but she had her letters and she wrote at dawn
when the fires had been built and the coffee pot perked.
On snowy evenings after the day's long list of chores done
she curled by the wood stove pen and pad in hand
the kerosene lamp glow haloing her blithe face
while her husband shook his head, sighing,
and turned back to his newspaper.

Every mail day was Christmastime,
every opened envelope a gift;
for in the ink she saw eyes and
in the feel of the paper she felt hands
and in the written words she heard voices, laughter, songs.

Even after the road pushed through,
with easy access to town and the treat of people,
she wrote to far away family and friends,
she wrote to far away family and friends,
she wrote to strangers who knew more about her life
and her love of the land than anyone.

She saved her legacy of letters,
lining them in boxes by name and date.
They became her reason for being,
the only thing she had to call her own
and in the end it was enough.

                    —for Virginia Bennett's ranch
                      wife in her poem "Tapestry of Knots"

KNEADING BREAD

Long before daylight, stove crackling,
coffee perking, I sprinkle yeast
on honeyed warm water, add salt
and oil, freshly ground whole wheat
flour which I stir and mix and fold
into fragrant bread dough.

I plunk it out onto an old
wood board while the wind woofs
hungrily at steam edged windows
and you toast your back
sip your morning cup and read about
falling cattle prices, costly feed.

In my worn sweats and slippers,
my hair twisted up in a slip-shod knot
I labor the dough with supple floured
fingers, the fine rhythm of work —
push-pull-turn, push-pull-turn,
transfiguring sticky wet into
elastic glossy smooth.

I feel your arms ease around me from
behind, your chest flannel full
against my curved back, your mouth
moist and breathy on my ear
moving wisps of escaped hair
tickling and teasing along my neck
sending spine shivers quivering to my toes.

Closing my eyes to this bliss kiss
kindness, your warmth weakens me,
melts me into an embrace that turns
me from the swollen dough to place
white hands upon your tan face,
leaves me wondering what it is
about kneading bread
that makes you need me.

WOOING THE WANTON MARE

After so many years afoot
I felt the mare would be mine:
hauled home in the back
of an old stock truck
she stood trembling at the far end
of the chewed pole corral, black
as a burnished raven's wing.

Oh! The names he called her flew
from his mouth like hot spit,
while she whirled and ran dust clouds,
tucked her head tight in a corner
and kicked, righteously, heels high,
until, he left in disgust, flinging halter
down in the powder fine manure dirt.

When he was gone I stole down
to see her, sat on the top pole
and talked her pinned ears up, her
nostrils open, so fluttery they moved
like moths against the night of her nose,
until at last she came to me on her own,
her deep eyes wide with the weight
of danger, her dark face softened
by a little crooked star.

Once saddled she rode like a willow
bending in the breeze, pliant, at ease,
everything in her alert, anxious,
as giving and willing as a ready woman.
That she would come to me but never to him
rubbed us raw as a gall, irritating our flesh
like an unanswerable ache.

Everything broke loose with my going:
my greatest regret after so many years
of giving in was leaving the mare,
her fine head hung over the gate
watching me drive away in the rain.

—for Sis

SUNDERANCE

I wondered what could creak
and groan, a moan so wholly human
I searched the frozen trees for sound,
for soul or shadow that unbound
would tell me who was there, invisible,
in April's early morning air.

I stood stock-still and listened hard,
so hard I heard my breath escape,
a little held back whispered shush,
the trackless hush of raven's rushing
wings that caught a rising drift of wind
below the ridge's rough and rocky face.

There, again, a pained and weary cry,
a piercing sigh from unseen place,
I tuned my inner ear and heard the hardened
heart of something break. So still,
so soft and warm, the slant of new born light,
the sun's incomprehensible injury to ice.

THE ALIENS

In the Sixties,
I was a peace freak —
helped shut a campus down
without firing a shot.
& ever since it seems
I'm doing battle —
especially in my head.

I've fought drought
barb wire, cattle thieves
down markets & my relatives,
the Army Corps of Engineers,
surface mining profiteers,
alcohol, & the IRS,
two ex-wives,
& yes, Bukowski,
there are people
        out there
who go through life with
very little friction
or distress —
they die an easy sleep.

Baxter says I'm *cursed*
to find meaning
in the chaos of men's minds,
inscribes it kindly
inside *Croutons on A Cowpie,*
Vol. #2 — & he knows
        the gray battlefield —
& in the debris
finds his line of levity
by staring the tragic beast down
eye to eye
in the mirror.

Trudy says that Salinas says
that we have no eyelids —
that disfigured so, we cannot blink
even in our dreams. Yet
there is rest at the end,
peace for a moment in a poem
like the dawn that now
    invades this silent canyon
    with the prehistoric silhouette
    of a Great Blue Heron
    dragging his feet
    in the light.

ONE, APRIL

The only sense I can perceive
is that the threshold opens vast
that some shall enter less naive
where truth is known but never asked.

It runs between each molecule
that touches close and wanders far—
we spin in space, the wise and fool
to redirect our shooting star.

The wildest song that hums the least,
the tune the deaf can turn to dance
must run spring pure and unpoliced
to cut its way with circumstance.

I am the raven, I am part crow,
a coyote's wit to wile on breeze,
the rock that floats in air below—
I am the quaking in the leaves.

It comes with April's warm and wet
and pumping sap beneath thin bark
that strains to reach and press regret
to shapes of strength without remark

and if the cloud can hold my weight
and if my soul walks burdenless
I leave no track in endless fate.
My each step whispers—answers, "Yes."

TO HAVE A MAN

Doubt she's ever needed
A man for much
since she was twelve —
doubt she needs
much more
than someone
to fish the mouse out
of the dog's water —
someone she can trust
to wash his hands.

TWENTY-SIXTH WINTER

I've wanted to squeeze
despair into thin air,
discharge bold charity
with my *Remington*
muzzle to her ear,
blast gray suffering
from this fleshless, ratty hide
tight as a drum
over Willow Buena's bones
half-a-dozen times
when the shadows climbed
up canyon evenings
each September
to only let her go
another winter
with each memory
in her one soft eye,
the other in a cloud.
And were I young again —
she'd be gone.

Her neck is softer
beneath the halter
as I lead her out
of her retirement, away
from the fretting mules
she's babysat
the past six years
    & I think of my father's step
    as it slides along the furrow,
    led up & down the orchard row
by something
    I can't quite see
in me.
    Another man,
    another horse,

another time
would have let nature claim her,
graze until gravity pulled her down
some frosty night
    to be licked & chewed,
    melt away,
    forgotten carrion.

The ridgeline of her spine is hard
to look at
    this close to the house
    in the only spot of green.
She trains us,
    rattles the bucket
    earlier each dawn
    as if she could
    bring the sun.

AFTER THIS

The rain came though we didn't
smell it coming on the wind
because of the smoke. The forests
were burning, there were bright
sunsets in the west but that's summer —
if not lightning then some
nut with a match, some slob
of a camper who hacks
at lodgepole until it drips
sap, then tosses beer cans
under the picnic table and lets
the campfire smolder. We might
not have noticed at all
because of the fires but
the clouds settled in over smoke
and the rain rattled the fiberglass
roof of the shed and the children
danced and after this,
we could not leave.

FINDING THE TRAIL

It's there behind that first patch
of huckleberries, between Douglas
fir and scrubby yew. It may be
a deer trail, or elk—doesn't
matter really—they all
travel this way. It's what
you have been looking for,
beginning near berries you can
find with your nose and ending
where you can't imagine.

AUGUST

My cousin was five.
We walked with her to the granaries
to ask the men if they needed food,
to ask if they needed water to drink.
It was harvest. The grass
was dry and crackly. The crop
was pretty good.

When we passed the grease house
we heard the rattle, and
I pulled my cousin's arm,
flipped her belly-down
behind me. She didn't cry,
and my mother told me to run
for the hoe.

She cut three times
to separate the head from
its coiled body, then carried the head
on the blade of the hoe. The mouth
opened and closed, the fangs
bit into air. My mother dug a hole
beside the cottonwood trees
and buried the open mouth there.

She told us to leave that place
alone, told us to watch
so the dogs wouldn't dig.

NAMES OF HORSES

All winter your brute shoulders strained against collars, padding
and steerhide over the ash hames, to haul
sledges of cordwood for drying through spring and summer,
for the Glenwood stove next winter, and for the simmering range.

In April you pulled cartloads of manure to spread on the fields,
dark manure of Holsteins, and knobs of your own clustered with oats.
All summer you mowed the grass in meadow and hayfield, the
mowing machine clacketing beside you, while the sun walked high in the morning;

and after noon's heat, you pulled a clawed rake through the same acres,
gathering stacks, and dragged the wagon from stack to stack,
and the built hayrack back, up hill to the chaffy barn,
three loads of hay a day, hanging wide from the hayrack.

Sundays you trotted the two miles to church with the light load
of a leather quartertop buggy, and grazed in the sound of hymns.
Generation on generation, your neck rubbed the window sill
of the stall, smoothing the wood as the sea smooths glass.

When you were old and lame, when your shoulders hurt bending to graze,
one October the man who fed you and kept you, and harnessed you every morning,
led you through corn stubble to sandy ground above Eagle Pond,
and dug a hole beside you where you stood shuddering in your skin,

and lay the shotgun's muzzle in the boneless hollow behind your ear,
and fired the slug into your brain, and felled you into your grave,
shoveling sand to cover you, setting goldenrod upright above you,
where by next summer a dent in the ground made your monument.

For a hundred and fifty years, in the pasture of dead horses,
roots of pine trees pushed through the pale curves of your ribs,
yellow blossoms flourished above you in autumn, and in winter
frost heaved your bones in the ground—old toilers, soil makers:

O Roger, Mackerel, Riley, Ned, Nellie, Chester, Lady Ghost.

HAYING: A FOUR-PART DEFINITION

I

When I was fourteen, my father bought a new John Deer 420
for me to drive. I'm thirty-four.
Some summers I've missed:
away at other jobs, married, teaching.
But I'm home for now.
For the twentieth spring he hitches up the mower,
mows the big yard, stops to sharpen sickles, straighten
sections, grease zerks.
Impatient, he begins before he's ready,
plunges in. When he's made the first land
he stops the tractor, grins, says "I usually drive it in third"
(so do I, I growl for the twentieth year)
pours himself some coffee.
I mow around the field in diminishing concentric squares
trying to write a poem about haying.

II

On the first round: alfalfa's purple smell.
On the third: redwing blackbirds fly up, screeching.
On the fourth: the cupped nest swings
from three plants; *on the fifth*: four chicks,
openmouthed, ride the nest down to die.
On the sixth: I remember the first time. They cheeped
while I carried the nest off the field. Two redwings
fluttered where it had stood. They never went near it;
a buzzard did. *On the tenth*: damp heat induces sleep.
On the twelfth: I watch the sickle slashing.
On the thirteenth: remember a story. A neighbor caught
his pants leg in the power takeoff. When his sons saw
the circling tractor he was a bloody lump, baseball-size.
On the fourteenth: calculate the temperature at
one hundred ten. The first hour ends.

On the twenty-eighth round: an eagle circles up the grove,
pursued by blackbirds. I think of the poem again:
seeking words for the heat, the pain between my shoulder blades,
the sweat bee stinging under my arm. For fierce hot time.
On the fortieth: I think of water. *On the forty-second*:
the sickle hits a fawn; his bleat pierces the tractor's chug
like cold water on a dusty throat. He lurches off.
There's no way to see them in the deep grass,
no way to miss. Still, we never tell my mother.
I begin to lose track, listening for loose bolts,
but around sixty my father finishes hitching up the rake,
waves me in for coffee. The second hour ends.

III

hay 1. n. Grass or other plants such as clover or alfalfa,
cut and dried for fodder. Slang. A trifling amount of money.
Used only in negative phrases, especially in "that ain't hay."

IV

Today I mowed ten acres of hay, laid
twenty tons of alfalfa down, raked
it into windrows for my father to stack
this afternoon. Tomorrow he'll gesture
to the two stacks and say, "Well,
we've started haying." In a month
the two of us will put up eighty tons;
by August perhaps one hundred ten.
Hay for the cattle against winter, pitched
out in the snow for their slow chewing, snow
blowing among the stems, drifting on their backs.

BUTCHERING THE CRIPPLED HEIFER

First:
    aim the pistol at her ear. Stand close.
    She chews slowly, eyes closed. Fire.
    She drops. Kicks. Sighs.
    Cut her throat and stand back.
    Blood bubbles and steams.

Then:
    wrap chain around each ankle,
    spread the back legs with a singletree.
    The tractor growls, lifting;
    the carcass sways.

Next:
    drive the knife point in,
    open the belly like tearing cloth,
    the blade just under the skin.
    Cut around the empty udder.
    Don't puncture the stomach.
    Sheathe the knife and reach in.
    Wrap your bare arms around the slick guts.
    Press your face against warm flesh.
    Find the ridge of backbone; tear the
    membranes loose. Hold the anus shut;
    pull hard until the great blue stomach bag
    spills into the tub at your feet.
    Jerk the windpipe loose with a sucking moan,
    her last sound.

Straighten:
    Breathe blood-scent, clean digested grass.
    Plunge one arm into the tub, cut loose the heart,
    and squeeze the last clots out; slice the liver
    away from the green gall, put it all in cool water.
    Eat fresh liver and onions for supper,
    baked heart tomorrow.

Finally:
    Cut off the head and feet,
    haul them and the guts to the pasture:
    coyotes will feast tonight.

Then:
    pull the skin taut with one hand,
    slice the spider web of tissue with care.
    Save the tail for soup.
    Drape the hide on the fence.

Let her hang:
    sheet-wrapped, through three cool October days,
    while leaves yellow and
    coyotes howl thanksgiving.

Cut her up:
    bring one quarter at a time to the kitchen table.
    Toss bones into the big soup kettle
    to simmer, the marrow sliding out. Chunk
    scraps, pack them in canning jars.
    Cut thick red steaks, wrap them in white paper,
    labeled for the freezer.

Make meat:
    worship at a bloody altar, knives singing praises
    for the heifer's health, for flesh she made
    of hay pitched at forty below zero last winter.

Your hands are red with her blood,
slick with her fat.

You know
where your next meal is coming from.

BEEF EATER

I have been eating beef hearts
all my life.
I split the smooth maroon shape
lengthwise,
open it like a diagram, chambers exposed.
I cut tough white membranes off valves,
slice onions over the heart,
float it in water,
boil it tender.
I chop prunes, apricots, mushrooms
to mix with dry bread,
sage from the hillside.
I pack the crevices full,
nail the heart together,
weave string around the nails.

Gently,
I lift the full heart
between my hands,
place it in the pan
with its own blood, fat, juices.
I roast that heart
at three hundred fifty degrees
for an hour or two.
Often I dip pan juices,
pour them lovingly over the meat.
When I open the oven,
the heart throbs
in its own golden fat.

I thicken the gravy with flour,
place the heart with love
on my Grandmother's ironstone platter,
slice it evenly from the small end;
pour gravy over it all,
smile as I carry it to the table.

My friends have begun to notice my placid air,
which they mistake for serenity.
Yesterday a man remarked on my large brown eyes,
my long eyelashes,
my easy walk.

I switched my tail at him
as if he were a fly,
paced
deliberately
away.

WHAT THE FALCON SAID

Flat on his back, feathers bloody,
surrounded by drooling cats,
the young falcon hissed,
clacked his beak, clawed air.
His feathers were bloody;
one cat licked a bleeding ear.
Falcon's yellow eyes didn't blink
when I picked him up
like a handful of springs,
like a grenade with the pin pulled.
None of the blood was his.

I put him high in a cedar tree.
He clutched the branch and panted,
glared at me,
then shot straight up like a bullet.
Next day, on my horse, I saw
a redwing blackbird whistling on a post
explode in the middle of a fluid run of song.
The falcon shot away, clutching the corpse.
He screeched once but I heard what he said:

Don't expect pretty lies from me.
I know my job.
You saved me from the cats
so I could live.
I kill to eat.
So do the cats.

So do you.

HANDS

The words won't come right from my hands
in spring. The fields are full
of baby calves, tufts of hay, bawling cows.
My brain is full—but words won't come.
Sometimes when I'm in the truck,
leading heifers to spring grass, I find a stub
of pencil, tear a piece from a cake sack,
and make notes, listening to the curlews'
wolf whistle. A barb tore that knuckle,
shutting a gate without my gloves. The blood
blister came when someone slammed a gate
on the branding table; I tore the fingernail
fixing a flat. The poems are in the scars,
and in what I will recall of all this, when
my hands are too broken to do it anymore.

Instead of a pencil my hands,
knotted like old wood, grip a pitchfork,
pitching hay to cows; blister on the handles of a tiller. Slick
with milk and slobber, they hold a calf,
push the cow's teat into his mouth,
feel his sharp teeth cut my fingers—
another scar. From my hands pours cake
for the yearlings, seed for garden
that will feed my family.

My hands become my husband's, weathering
into this job he chose by choosing me; my father's,
broken and aged, still strong as when
he held me on my first horse. All night,
while my body sleeps, my hands
keep weaving some pattern I do not recognize:
waving to blackbirds and meadowlarks,
skinning a dead calf, picking hay seeds from my hair
and underwear, building fires. Deftly, they butcher
a chicken with skill my brain does not recall.

Maybe they are no longer mine but Grandmother's,
back from the grave with knowledge in their bones
and sinews, hands scarred as the earth they came from
and to which they have returned.

When my grandmother was dying, when
the body and brain were nearly still
for the first time in eighty years, she snatched
the tubes from her arms. At the end,
her hands wove the air, setting the table,
feeding farmhands, sewing patches. Her hands kept
weaving the air,
weaving the strands
she took with her
into the dark.

MY LAST WILL AND TESTAMENT

Being of sound body and mind,
I speak to you who will inherit,
though you were never part of me.

I give you grass roots wound in earth's breast,
coyotes singing in wind,
meadowlarks flashing in the grass,
buffalo shaking the world with his bellow,
plowing with his hooves.
I give you back what our ancestors had.
You earn the land
after your name is on the title.
The sacraments of inheritance
require payment in blood and sweat.
If you only accept, you lose everything.

To hold it, you must fight
the plan to dump sewage in the creek,
fight the scheme to dump nuclear waste,
creating jobs
for people desperate enough to take them.

Fight the silence of the frozen land,
struggle to lift tons of baled hay,
fight for the lives of cows
made stupid by pain;
fight fire in winter grass,
stand helpless as hail booms on the roof.

Even if you are homeless, landless,
beware this bequest;
look this gift in its barbed teeth.
If you've never felt the wind
breathe in your lungs,
earth's blood singing in yours,
think before you accept this freedom,
this prison.

I will be gone.
But I, who have no heir,
speak to you in my blood, and yours.
One day a hawk will fall
through blue air to eye you from a fencepost,
a sego lily will raise its fluted face
beside your path.

COFFEE CUP CAFÉ

Soon as the morning chores are done,
cows milked, pigs fed, kids packed
off to school, it's down to the café
for more coffee and some soothing
conversation.

"If it don't rain pretty soon, I'm
just gonna dry up and blow away."

"Dry? This ain't dry. You don't know
how bad it can get. Why, in the Thirties
it didn't rain any more than this for
(breathless pause)   six years."

"I heard Johnson's lost ninety head of calves
in that spring snowstorm. They
were calving and heading for home
at the same time and they just walked
away from them."

"Yeah and when the cows
got home, half of them died
of pneumonia."

"I ain't had any hay on me since that hail
last summer; wiped out my hay crop, all
my winter pasture, and then the drouth
this spring. Don't know what I'll do."

"Yeah, but this is nothing yet.
Why in the Thirties the grasshoppers came
like hail and left nothing green on the ground.
They ate fenceposts, even. And the dust, why
it was deep as last winter's snow drifts,
piled against the houses. It ain't bad here yet,
and when it does come, there won't be so many of us
having coffee."

So for an hour they cheer each other, each story
worse than the last, each face longer. You'd think
they'd throw themselves under their tractors
when they leave, but they're bouncy as a new calf,
caps tilted fiercely into the sun.

They feel better, now they know
somebody's having a harder time
and that men like them
can take it.

GIVE US RAIN!

Don't we wait for rain in this dry country
licking down sweet wild kisses,
pretending it's not our heart's desire?

If rain was a person
we'd have given it up long ago as shiftless,
a worthless uncle, a tawdry aunt
—we've had both—
and still, when they come walking up the road
suitcase swinging,
hat cocked to shade one eye,
we beam a smile—the mirror of their own,
hear stories of their roaming,
sticking our tired old feet deeper into the sucking earth
that owns us,
our callused hands deeper in our pockets
where nothing jingles.
They whisk off too soon,
just a scent of store perfume on the pillow
pressed to my face.

I can't help but notice the persuasion of the clouds,
calves playing extra frisky, and that smell
—directly after
hope is all I know.

Light, it pit-a-pats on the barn roof like kittens playing.
Then it comes swifting down
holy water blessing the meadows alive   us alive.
Pretty soon it's pounding and my chest is tight.

Colts dance to the hammering on the tin,
pulling back against their halter ropes with white rimmed eyes.
Cattle buck and run to the trees, us to the porch.

Oh! We've missed you, rain!   Give us more!
Fill the tanks!

Lap the banks!
Wake the seeds!
Even weeds!
Drown the fish!

More hay!   Meadows jumping!
Turn those skinny old cows into butterballs!

Don't you know how happy we are to see you   beautiful old rain?
God!   We are happy!

SWANS

I let the swans float gently
on the blue gray sheen of the lake
though my secret wish is to be among them
grooming my own slim feathers.

The water is beneath.
Their black webbed strokes move them.
The sky is above.
Strong wings keep them moving there.

And when it is time
they rise above the lip of the lake.
High up the land and trees and water fade.
The earth is a tan and blue haze.

They see nothing but the simple air
and draw forward.
Some water clings to them
and some sky.

THE MAN SHOEING A HORSE AND HIS LITTLE GIRL

He whirled those blue eyes on me
    flat blue eyes
    bottomless eyes
    where the pupil had shrunk up so he was only seeing through that
pinhole
    screwing me down like a microscope seeing into me past awkward
structural uprights, joist and 2x4, past electrical wires running, past gray
puttied pipes, past insulation, wall board, paint, plaster, and chimney into
the real center—blueprint where angles could be altered to add or subtract
things, and I felt myself shrinking, all jellied with no legs to run

    but those eyes
    in that face flushed red by his frustration and the hoof ripped
through his knees
    seemed to wash calm
    the pupil coiled out and was the dark seeing center
    with the thin blue wall
    no more x-ray vision

    and those blue eyes
    ran over me like warm honey
    smeared me
    the rasping palm
    soft
    smoothed me out so I wasn't sorry anymore I asked the question
    and he

    in that voice

    I could pull on and wear

    spoke

PLAYING AT DOCTOR

Poor old broken legged ewe,
the flop of it wrings my stomach,
the grate climbs my spine like a stair.
Three strong legs are tied
so I can mend the one that snapped
when the shearer yanked you under the curtain.
Your eyes are closed. Your breath
blows the dirt smooth as I wind the gauze
up and down, up and down the cedar splints.
Without a scan I find alignment with my fingers
and hope your muscles will pull the bones tight.
I roll you to your feet and fight you to a stall
where you stand on three legs and blame me for your pain.
Your plaster stiffens my hands to hooves.

IN THE EVENING AUTUMN

As I rode out to check cows calving
the light came across the meadow low
soft
and in it
I could see a shimmering blanket of cobwebs
moving in the breeze
like the surface of water.

The whole of the meadow
under billowing silk.

While I go about my singular life
an army
of small spiders
has set about to hold this entire world together
in a veil of fine silver strands.

I FIX THE FENCE — THE FENCE FIXES ME

The fence I patched ran away
   rolled a week ahead.
   Ahead.
My horse along for company, we sang
   my horse and me
   Yippie-ti-yi-yo
   so my horse and I would know
   this work — this fence, assigned to me
   was just a lark,
   for I could see
   there were no other ones this free,
   just him and me
   and air
   that danced with Spring
   going in
   and loaded down with dreary Winter
   freed me with each sigh.
   Good-bye.

Fence work is pointed sharp,
   makes me look tight at wire frayed,
   staples sprung, wood posts splayed.
As morning raced on mended wire
   I began to tire
   of all this freedom, and my horse's songs ran dry.
   Spring's snap became a plod,
   the sun burned hot,
   the water gone. I thought of home and company
   then felt the wire
   take a bite of me.
   I looked smaller still to see
   how deep a barb can tear, when
   bluebirds —
   bluebirds, blue as sky
   bluer than a baby's eye
   blue as love's reply —
   flit,
   not fly

from sage to sage
on flicker wings, and sing
Cheer. Cheer lee churn
each one in turn.

Well—
what is there for a buckaroo
to do
but blush a bit
at nature's wit
and blow a kiss
to birds so blue
they leave the sky behind.

DEAR CHILD

We gathered the desert in June
  to brand calves born since turn-out
  to move them up to the mountain
    with the feed.

June is hot on the desert.
Days are long on the desert.

Ride a wide circle,
    gather toward a gate,
      brand the afternoon away,
        trot to camp
          and supper
            and bed.

I worried about Katie,
    our tiny girl of seven,
But she pushed Smokey near a rock,
    shinnied up his old leg
      and rode out among the buckaroos.

The sun came out hot
    as Katie and I rode across Butcher Flat,
    swung toward Sarvis
      pushing cattle in front of us.
I sent her to the ridges
    into sudden draws
      for a break from the pecking along behind.
Always, some small calves
    keeping up,
      little hocks brushing,
      tails swinging,
        on the long trail
        to be branded.

In the early afternoon
    we saw the rest bunched
        through the dust choking us
        and heat waves dancing,
        smoke drifting hotter,
            the branding started.
Katie croaked, "I'm thirsty."
"I know."
    But it was in my
    Words-of-wisdom period
    and I said,
        "There's no use complaining, dear child.
          We're all thirsty
          and we're all hungry
          and we're all tired.
        We have to finish the work.
        When the work is done
          we can rest.
        You don't hear anyone else say,
          'I'm thirsty.'
        They all are
          but they don't say it.
            Saying it makes us all twice as thirsty.
        Hold on, we'll be there soon."

We finished the day.
Trotting back to camp
    Katie was strong in the middle,
        learning how buckaroos only tease those they like.

She had a water fight in the spring before supper,
    ate like a field hand,
    fell asleep sitting up.

When I tucked her into the bedroll
    I kissed her sunburned cheeks and said,
        "You were perfect today."
    And in her own child's wisdom she said,
        "No, Mom. Not perfect
            . . . almost perfect."

One day soon
    to her small boy
        she'll say,
            "There's no use complaining,
                    dear child."

LOVE LETTERS

"Wow!" was written in the dust
    on the bedside table.

The dawn and I blushed together
    as your spurs
    ching
    chinged
    around the kitchen
    and you started the fire.

I stretched full length
    on the cool smoothness
    of the sheets,

a kept woman
    a moment longer.

Within an hour's time
    we'll be ahorseback
    in a long trot
    to some distant blue mountain
    hunting cows.

I'll carry your message
    close
    knowing there will come a day
I would give a year of my life
    for that . . .
        "Wow!"

SO MANY HORSES

At sundown the old man stands alone
and thinks of the horses, dead and gone,
that plodded the road with loads of hay
and worked their lives out day on day.

So many horses, so many years.
He smells their sweat and faintly hears
the ghostly blow of their patient breath
upon his sleeve. He feels them snuff

and gently nuzzle gifts of grain
cupped in the hollow of his hand.
So many horses, dead so long,
he leads in dreams as night comes on.

THE BARN

In the black barn, swallows sleep
like old songs.
But cows are wakeful.
Someone enters
through the tired wooden doors,
a man with a lantern.
He forks hay into ancient mangers,
and the cows gaze at him
in their silent ancient tongue.
Like a prayer, dawn seeps
into the boards
of the barn.
The man reaches to touch
one plank.

WHISPERS

Year after year, the cowboy whispers
all he knows
into the ear of his horse.

TO THE WILD PONY

I dip my hands into the bin
and lift them full of
                    oats
redolent of all
the wild fields you have
known.

When I breathe their fumes
I am gone
to some lone wild
                    field.

Only my hands are here still
brimming with sweet
oats.

Come
dip your soft lips
                    deep.

AMANDA IS SHOD

The way the cooked shoes sizzle
dropped in a pail of cold water
the way the coals in the portable forge
die out like hungry eyes
the way the nails go in aslant
each one the tip of a snake's tongue

and the look of the parings
after the farrier's knife
has sliced through.

I collect them
four marbled white C's
as refined as petrified wood
and dry them to circles of bone
and hang them away on my closet hook

lest anyone cast a spell on Amanda.

THE AGNOSTIC SPEAKS TO HER HORSE'S HOOF

Come, frog, reveal yourself.
Surface out of the poultice
the muck and manure pack.
Make your miraculous V to stand up.
Show me as well the tickle place
that cleft between.

The Good Book says a man's life
is as grass the wind passes over
and is gone.
According to the *National Geographic*
the oceans will lie down dead
as cesspools in sixty years.

Let us ripen in our own way—
I with my back to the trunk
of a butternut that has caught
the fatal red canker
and on my knee
this skillet of your old foot.

The hoofpick is God's instrument
as much as I know of Him.

In my hands let it raise
your moon, Amanda, your nerve bone.
Let us come to the apocalypse complete without splinter or stone.
Let us ride out on four iron feet.

THINKING OF DEATH
AND DOGFOOD

Amanda, you'll be going
to Alpo or to Gaines
when you run out of luck;
the flesh flensed from your bones
your mammoth rib cage rowing
away to the renderer's
a dry canoe on a truck

while I foresee my corpse
slid feet first into fire
light as the baker's loaf
to make of me at least
a pint of potash spoor.
I'm something to sweeten the crops
when the clock hand stops.

Amanda, us in the woods
miles from home, the ground
upending in yellow flutes
that open but make no sound.
Ferns in the mouth of the brute,
chanterelles in the woman's sack . . .
what do I want for myself
dead center, bareback
on the intricate harp of your spine?
All that I name as mine

with the sure slow oxen of words:
feed sacks as grainy as boards
that air in the sun. A boy
who is wearing my mother's eyes.
Garlic to crush in the pan.
The family gathering in.
Already in the marsh
the yearling maples bleed
a rich onrush. Time slips
another abacus bead.

Let it not stick in the throat
or rattle a pane in the mind.
May I leave no notes behind
wishful, banal or occult
and you, small thinker in
the immensity of your frame,
may you be caught and crammed
midmouthful of the best grain
when the slaughterer's bullet slams
sidelong into your brain.

FEEDING TIME

Sunset. I pull on
parka, boots, mittens, hat,
cross the road to the paddock.
Cat comes,
the skinny, feral tom
who took us on last fall.
Horses are waiting.
Each enters his box
in the order they've all
agreed on, behind my back.
Cat supervises from the molding cove.
Hay first. Water next. Grain last.
Check thermometer: seven degrees.
Check latches. Leave.

The sky
goes purple, blotched with red.
Feed dog next.
I recross the road to the woodshed.
Snappish moment with cat
but no real contest.
Wag, wag, kerchunk! The plate
is polished. Dog
grovels his desire
to go inside, lie like a log
by the fire.

Two above.
Above, it's gray
with meager afterglow.
Feed birds next.
I wade by way
of footprint wells through deep snow
to cylinders on trees.
Cat follows
observing distribution
of sunflower seeds.

Checks out each heel-toe
I've stepped in, in case
something he needs,
something small and foolish lurks.
No luck.

Penultimate,
cat gets
enormous supper:
chicken gizzards! Attacks
these like a cougar
tearing, but not in haste.
Retires to barn loft
to sleep in the hay,
or pretends to. Maybe
he catches dessert this way.

Now us,
Dear One. My soup, your bread
in old blue bowls that have withstood
thirty years of slicings and soppings.
Where are the children
who ate their way through helpings
of cereals and stews
to designs of horse, pig,
sheep on view
at the bottom of the dish?
Crying, *when I grow up,*
children have got their wish.

It's ten below.
The house dozes.
The attic stringers cough.
Time that blows on the kettle's rim
waits to carry us off.

LE COURSIER DE JEANNE D'ARC

You know that they burned her horse
before her. Though it is not recorded,
you know that they burned her Percheron
first, before her eyes, because you

know that story, so old that story,
the routine story, carried to its
extreme, of the cruelty that can make
of what a woman hears *a silence,*

that can make of what a woman sees
a lie. She had no son for them to burn,
for them to take from her in the world
not of her making and put to its pyre,

so they layered a greater one in front of
where she was staked to her own —
as you have seen her pictured sometimes,
her eyes raised to the sky. But they were

not raised. This is yet one of their lies.
They were not closed. Though her hands
were bound behind her, and her feet were
bound deep in what would become fire,

she watched. Of greenwood stakes
head-high and thicker than a man's waist
they laced the narrow corral that would not
burn until flesh had burned, until

bone was burning, and laid it thick
with tinder—fatted wicks and sulfur,
kindling and logs—and ran a ramp
up to its height from where the gray horse

waited, his dapples making of his flesh
a living metal, layers of life
through which the light shone out
in places as it seems to through the flesh

of certain fish, a light she knew
as purest, coming, like that, from within.
Not flinching, not praying, she looked
the last time on the body she knew

better than the flesh of any man, or child,
or woman, having long since left the lap
of her mother—the chest with its
perfect plates of muscle, the neck

with its perfect prow-like curve,
the hindquarters'—pistons—powerful cleft
pennoned with the silk of his tail.
Having ridden as they did together

—those places, that hard, that long—
their eyes found easiest that day
the way to each other, their bodies
wedded in a sacrament unmediated

by man. With fire they drove him
up the ramp and off into the pyre
and tossed the flame in with him.
This was the last chance they gave her

to recant her world, in which their power
came not from God. Unmoved, the Men
of God began watching him burn, and better,
watching her watch him burn, hearing

the long mad godlike trumpet of his terror,
his crashing in the wood, the groan
of stakes that held, the silverblack hide,
the pricked ears catching first

like dryest bark, and the eyes.
And she knew, by this agony, that she
might choose to live still, if she would
but make her sign on the parchment

they would lay before her, which now
would include this new truth: that it
did not happen, this death in the circle,
the rearing, plunging, raging, the splendid

armor-colored head raised one last time
above the flames before they took him
—like any game untended on the spit—into
their yellow-green, their blackening red.

A THOUSAND GENUFLECTIONS

Winter mornings when I call her,
out of falling snow she trots
into view, her tail and mane
made flame by movement, carrying,
as line and motion, back into air
her shape and substance—like fire
into heat into light, turns
the candle takes, burning.
And her head—her senses,
every one is a scout sent out
ahead of her, behind, beside:
her eye upon me, over the distance,
her ear, its million listeners,
delicate and vast her nose, her mouth,
her voice upon me, closing the distance.
I could just put the buckets down
and go, but I kneel to hold them
as she eats, as she drinks, to be
this close. For something of myself
lives here, stripped of the knowing
that is not knowing, a single thing
from the least webbed tissues
of the heart straight out to the tips
of the guardhairs that shimmer off
beyond my sight into air, the grasses,
grain, the water, light.
I've come like this each day
for years across the hard winters,
seeing a figure for the thing itself,
divine—appetite and breath,
flesh and attention. This morning
her presence asks of me: *And might
you be your body? Might we be
not the figure, but the thing itself?*

GIRL FROM LYNN BATHES HORSE!!

1100 pounds, more or less, the mare
high-steps a trot on a short circle
—two feet of line from the hand
of the Tenement Kid who never outgrew
the wish to be able to do this
to the head of the horse who never
watched TV, never saw the Lone Ranger
or Hoppy, never read about Smoky or
Flicka, Black Beauty or King of the Wind,
and so cannot possibly know that the only
thing the two of them need to perform
this difficult, dangerous act together

is *love*, the kind between cowgirl and pony,
infused as the Garden's knowing. To hell
with experience, instruction, example,
coin of the grownup world. You don't
really need what you don't really own.

In her off hand the stiff hose kinks,
coiling underfoot as the mare circles,
hating the green snake, the water that spurts,
urging her faster, crosser at every turn,
in the tight well of mud, in the slick-
footing'd flood of the yard. *It's a lot like
washing a car,* she quips, as a shod hoof
flies out when the wet slaps horse privates —
It's always like something else, this life

for which squirting a half-ton of horse-in-hand
on the strength of a nine-year-old's metaphysics
is a figure for all the rest, for the morning
by morning invention of a self
in the laboratory of unmarked chemicals.

Childhood is the barrel they give you
to go over the falls in. Whatever you get to take
with you in it can't be bigger or sharper

than an idea. It must be that fall, clenched
in a kid's fist (as earth expresses a diamond)
that transforms it from simply Some Dumb Thing
to Some Dumb Thing that is magic,
the *fifth essence*, perhaps, what the alchemists
knew lay latent in every thing. Even the least.
Even the most ridiculous.

BUCKED

Balanced for that instant
in midair, I watched
his rump, in white slow-motion
rise — heart-cleft, perfect —
to deliver the awesome blow.

How beautiful the muscles
of the world in their uses!
Great limbs of trees, waves
scaling seawalls, the moon's
dreadful flex on everything,

heart valves and minute
vessels, the spiraled cues
for weakness that I pass on
to my children: of which
might one ask to be spared?

ON HORSEBACK

—for the McFauns

We are only walking.
This is not the romance
of horseback riding:
your mane, which is short
and scraggly, sticks out
like a hedge of cowlicks
or merely flops off to the side.
Nothing is flying, trans-
porting, transcendent.

Then we aren't a metaphor
for anything, Shawnee James,
little borrowed horse I learn on.
Your body is bent and dented
as the first car I owned,
the '52 Plymouth, brush-painted,
one walleye headlight
held in with masking tape.
And I am a comparable model.

But, cast off the road,
our shadow is travelling
across the cut stubble of October.
My hands have forgotten themselves,
as the shadow has forgotten them,
does not require them.
With your four legs, our two heads
find a balance.

A single thing in gray,
its many muscles flush and flexing
in everyday grace,
we move over the grass, as whole
as the shape anything makes, passing.
We are something going somewhere,
handsome and practical and proud.
We shake out our tail.

RIDING OUT AT EVENING

At dusk, everything blurs and softens.
From here out over the long valley,
the fields and hills pull up
the first slight sheets of evening,
as, over the next hour,
heavier, darker ones will follow.

Quieted roads, predictable deer
browsing in a neighbor's field, another's
herd of heifers, the kitchen lights
starting in many windows. On horseback
I take it in, neither visitor
nor intruder, but kin passing, closer
and closer to night, its cold streams
rising in the sugarbush and hollow.

Half-aloud, I say to the horse,
or myself, or whoever: let fire not come
to this house, nor that barn,
nor lightning strike the cattle.
Let dogs not gain the gravid doe, let the lights
of the rooms convey what they seem to.

And who is to say it is useless
or foolish to ride out in the falling light
alone, wishing, or praying,
for particular good to particular beings,
on one small road in a huge world?
The horse bears me along, like grace,

making me better than what I am,
and what I think or say or see
is whole in these moments, is neither
small nor broken. For up, out of
the inscrutable earth, have come my body
and the separate body of the mare:
flawed and aching and wronged. Who then
is better made to say *be well, be glad,*

or who to long that we, as one,
might course over the entire valley,
over all valleys, as a bird in a great embrace
of flight, who presses against her breast,
in grief and tenderness,
the whole weeping body of the world?

WITH THE HORSE IN THE WINTER PASTURE

Zero degrees, no wind, and barely
the January sun has begun to ripen.
You, who all day yesterday
brooked with your body
a brutal storm from the north,
now graze as amiably over the snow
and hay as if it were August.
Or more so: free of the flies, free
of the rider—bit, crop, and fetter.
What we endure need not turn us to stone,
insists the gray bird in the birch-on-blue,
who survives in her three least notes.
And so, today, I am victim
of nothing, nor am I mistress, just
hanging around the sun-catching corner
as if it were after school, a fool,
a woman carrying on like a girl.
I throw my arm over your withers
and bury my face in your neck:
white plush, pulse, smell
of woodsmoke. The child is alive
who prayed by her bed to die.

WE NEVER RODE THE JUDITHS

—for Ian Tyson

We never rode the Judiths when we were grey-wolf wild.
Never gathered Powder River, Palo Duro, or John Day.
No, we never rode the Judiths when their sirens preened and smiled.
And we'll never ride the Judiths before they carry us away.

Cowboys cut for sign on back trails to the days that used to be
Sorting, sifting through chilled ashes of the past.
Or focused on some distant star, out near eternity,
Always hoping that the next day will be better than the last.

Out somewhere in the future, where spring grass is growing tall,
We rosin up our hopes for bigger country, better pay.
But as the buckers on our buckles grow smooth-mouthed or trip and fall
We know tomorrow's draw ain't gonna throw no gifts our way.

And we never rode the Judiths when we were grey-wolf bold.
Never rode the Grande Ronde Canyon out north of Enterprise.
No we never rode the Judiths, and we know we're getting old
As old trails grow steeper, longer, right before our eyes.

My horses all are twenty-some . . . ain't no good ones coming on.
The deejays and the Nashville hands won't let ". . . Amazed" turn gold.
We're inclined to savor evening now. We usta favor dawn.
Seems we're not as scared of dyin' as we are of growing old.

I wish we'd a' rode the Judiths when we were grey-wolf wild.
And gathered Powder River, Palo Duro, and John Day.
But we never rode the Judiths when their sirens' songs beguiled
And we'll never ride the Judiths before they carry us away.

SOLD TO THE HIGHEST BIDDER

"Sold to the highest bidder!"
The gavel crashes down.
Another rural family
Goes shamblin' into town.

> Sold to the highest bidder
> Their dreams go down, dirt-cheap;
> Where every dream's a nightmare
> Endured in fitful sleep.

Sold to the highest bidder
The trinkets forged with tears,
Framed pictures on the bureau
Of graduation years.

> Sold to the highest bidder.
> To town go the crocks and jars,
> Just knick-knacks now, or planters
> In condos or fern bars.

Sold to the highest bidder,
The cowbell and milk pail.
"They're chic," observes a shallow voice,
"I'll hang them on a nail."

> "Sold to the highest bidder!"
> The gavel crashes down.
> Another rural family
> Goes shamblin' into town.

GRANDMOTHER'S FRENCH HOLLYHOCKS

They were probably planted there by the gate
Or along the fence of the watergap lot
Where the milk cows lazed and the work teams ate
Chicken-wired out of the garden plot.

Why! didn't she know they'd scatter around?
Their seeds infecting our vegetable garden.
Magenta blooms fought for fertile ground
Crowding and choking, begging no pardon

Of the carrots or beets in militant rows,
Cut down by the shrapnel of Gaulish genes,
From ambush, they fell like dominoes.
In retreat we skirmished to save the beans

For the canning jars, waiting empty and green,
Wide mouthed as grackles with demanding maws,
That would nourish during months snowy and lean,
When the hunger moon, grinning, flexed grizzled jaws.

"Foolish woman!" we thought, to be tempted by beauty.
"What could she be thinking?" so all of us said.
Our lives bound by the iron bands of duty,
Not frivolous flowers! Just beans, beef and bread.

Of course no one complained, not to her face.
She surely repented the sin of her ways.
Her silent apology mitigated disgrace,
But the shame of her weakness she bore all her days.

She was guilty, of course. More guilty were we.
For beauty in life has strong healing powers.
Fifty years later, I'm beginning to see
The value of Grandmother's beautiful flowers.

A WOMAN'S PLACE
—for Karla Gambill

"A woman's place is in the home." That always has made sense.
They're just not built for riding broncs, nor fixin' barbwire fence.
The "woman's place" is well-defined throughout the cowboy West,
Besides, it's our tradition. Our old ways have stood time's test.
There's lots of things that women do way better than a man.
They're a whiz at washing diapers, or with a frying pan.
Those ladies are a comfort when a man ain't feelin' prime,
So, for cookin' or for lookin', give me a woman every time.
I've always advocated the old values of the West.
I believe, just like gospel, that the old-time rules is best.

A few years back I put things off, like I'm inclined to do.
When branding time come rolling 'round—I didn't have a crew.
And this girl, I'll call her "Laurie," said she'd agree to lend a hand.
I thought she meant her husband! See, I didn't understand
That she meant *her*, you savvy now that I was in a bind.
I didn't want to break her heart. I couldn't be unkind.
She said she had these horses that needed lotsa miles.
I said we'd start at daylight. She says, "Great. And thanks," and smiles.
'Bout three o'clock next morning, while I'm still snoring hard,
I starts, and hears a creeping gooseneck ease into the yard.
We invites her in for breakfast, but she's already ate.
It's an hour and half to daybreak 'n I'm already late.
The crew shows up, but she's the one who gives me an assist
When Old Ranger tries to buck me off. She gathers cows I missed!
While I gees and haws Old Ranger, her horse rolls o'er his hocks.
She cuts us cowboys seven ways, 'n does it orthodox.
There ain't nothin' that that girl can't do! I'm feelin' like a dope.
At last in desperation, I says, "Laurie, wanta rope?"
She keeps six rasslers busy. We're all abustin' gut.
She even finds a branded bull that I forgot to cut.
For four long days she shows us how a real hand operates.
She rassles and gives shots and brands. She even "casterates"!
When we gets done I offer up to ride, to pay her back.

In the nicest way that she knows how, she lets me know: I lack
Some basic skills I never learned. My horses ain't the best.
They got more help than they can use. I prob'ly need a rest.

So:

"A woman's place is in the home," to me don't seem so strange,
Because I finally figured Laurie's "Home (is) On The Range."

MALCOLM AND THE STRANGLERS

I'm a fair, upstanding citizen,
    honest, trustingly true-blue,
But one time in my secret past,
    I joined a vigilante crew.

We had trailed a herd to Colstrip
    where the N.P. had a yard
And punched 'em into rail cars.
    It was hot and we'd worked hard.
My mother and Aunt Alice
    had fixed a scrumptious lunch
That the hands dispatched with relish
    after loading up the bunch.
My dad (or Uncle Evan) said,
    "Boys, lead our horses home.
We're hot 'n tired 'n sweaty;
    our backsides crave the foam
Of Chevrolet car seats, besides
    we'd be plumb insane
Not to post the buyer's check
    for the steers there on the train."
So, Duke took the reins of Peanuts
    and I led my dad's horse, Star.
We all hit the road for home,
    it wasn't all that far.
So as we're trotting homeward,
    right down the county road,
A car with California plates
    scatters gravel as it slowed
To a sliding stop amongst us
    and this family scrambles out.
They starts to snappin' pictures
    'n quizzin' Mac what we're about.
Though Malcolm's long suit's bullshit
    (plus an artful type of braggin'),

He deals 'em straight til they inquire
    on the empty mounts we're draggin'.
"We just caught and hung two rustlers,
    t'other side of that divide,
and we're fetchin' to their widows
    these two broncs they usta ride."
"You kids get in the car right now!"
    the woman volunteers.
"These men are killers! Don't look at them!
    And cover up your ears!"
The man backs up a step or two.
    "Is that legal?" he inquires.
"Far as I know," Mac says, and grins.
    "That's what the law requires."
"Are you lawmen then?" the dude asks Mac,
    as his knees begin to rattle.
"We're vigilantes," Malcolm says,
    "'n them bastards stole some cattle."
"Could I take some camera pictures
    of those rustlers in their tree?"
"Hell, they won't care," says Malcolm,
    "and it's sure Jake with me."

Next week, in rolls a deputy
    whose demeanor's sorta tense,
With a tale about two murders;
    says he's seekin' evidence.
Well, Malcolm, he confesses,
    concludin' California folks
Ain't got no sense of humor
    when it comes to cowboy jokes.
But somewhere out in California
    there's photographic dossiers
Of Malcolm and us Stranglers
    in our vigilante days.

RIDERS' BLOCK

Tonight they're trying, once again,
With pencils poised, impatient pen,
To scribe the ultimate in verse.
They write, erase; they chafe and curse
In roundup camp, in barroom smoke
To braid in rhyme the latest joke.
The quest to fill the current rage
For cowboy pomes, to mount the stage
In Elko, is their hearts' desire.
They writhe in rage beside the fire.
Each stanza's formed, in diagram,
In foreheads throbbing with iamb.
Prepared to drop each "G" in "ing."
Slick metaphors are poised to spring.
All they need's a topic, yet
Each mind is numb. They squirm and sweat.
They quick-draw blanks. They should be fannin'
Bull's-eyes aimed at Elder Cannon!
Why! They could rival Badger Clark!
If mental coils produced one spark
To light this black hole, filled with doubt.
But no! No mark, they missed him out.
To hell with humor! Nostalgia then?
A saga of bold saddlemen?
A cutting swipe at dudes? Or women?
Or bureaucrats? Their minds are swimmin'.
Damn Zarzyski, Michael Logan,
Who never lack a theme or slogan
Or inspiration for a rhyme.
What's their gimmick? Why's it I'm
Stuck here rimrocked, thinking zero,
When I could be a western hero
On Western Horseman's poet's page?
A sagebrush rhyming cowboy sage.
My powder's wet. The well is dry.
Calliope has passed me by.

Take heart, all you rhyming pards,
The West is filled with want-to bards
Just two quarts low of inspiration,
Filled tonight with great frustration.
Horse rider's block, you're right, 's a curse,
But pardner, there's one problem worse:
It's them that's got but zilch to say
But goes and writes 'em anyway.

THINGS OF INTRINSIC WORTH

Remember that sandrock on Emmells Crick
Where Dad carved his name in 'thirteen?
It's been blasted down into rubble
And interred by their dragline machine.
Where Fadhls lived, at the old Milar place,
Where us kids stole melons at night?
They'd 'dozed it up in a funeral pyre
Then torched it. It's gone alright.
The "C" on the hill, and the water tanks
Are now classified "reclaimed land."
They're thinking of building a golf course
Out there, so I understand.
The old Egan homestead's an ash pond
That they say is eighty feet deep.
The branding corral at the Douglas camp
Is underneath a spoil heap.
And across the crick is a tipple, now,
Where they load coal onto a train.
The Mae West Rock on Hay Coulee?
Just black-and-white snapshots remain.
There's a railroad loop and a coal storage shed
Where the bison kill site used to be.
The Guy place is gone; Ambrose's, too.
Beulah Farley's a ranch refugee.

But things are booming. We've got this new school
That's envied across the whole state.
When folks up and ask, "How's things goin' down there?"
I grin like a fool and say, "Great!"
Great God, how we're doin'! We're rollin' in dough,
As they tear and they ravage The Earth.
And nobody knows . . . or nobody cares . . .
About things of intrinsic worth.

BREAKER IN THE PEN

There's a thousand year old story
involving beasts and men.
With one of each we set the stage
and let the play begin.

Take Eohippus' grandson
now on middle fingernail,
and the world's most recent primate
with no vestige left of tail.

The first outweighs the second
eight times or maybe ten.
Nothing new this story of the horse
and the breaker in the pen.

At times he thinks he's crazy
other times he knows for sure
but centaur blood pumps through his
veins and there isn't any cure.

There are broncs that try his patience,
and those that test his skill.
Make him lie awake in nighttime,
make him almost lose his will.

There are stiffened, aching mornings
when he questions if he'll last,
cause the breaker's close to 50
while the broncs are still two-past.

No imaginary spider web
connects him to the brute,
just developed understanding,
maybe years in taking root.

A dozen broncs stand shivering,
the mist is rolling in,
there's a slicker on the top rail,
and a breaker in the pen.

He's a study in persistence,
even stubborn if you will—
can bend more often than he breaks
and tough, damn tough to kill.

Rumor runs he nursed on mare's milk,
some say he's into Zen;
truth is he lives and breathes the work
the breaker in the pen.

There are times he feels restricted
by the endless little rounds,
wishing he were on the cow crew
with the roundup sights and sounds.

But he's seen the cattle sorted
now the crew comes trotting in
astride the horses started
by the breaker in the pen.

He's not high on riding buckers
and disdains the use of quirt;
he's eaten quite a little more
than his fair share of dirt.

So he reads what's there before him,
trying hard to catch the signs;
instinct or intuition
gives him what's between the lines.

This psycho-cybernetic work
has often saved this hide,

but the moment comes with every horse
when he has to mount and ride.

So fearless (or in spite of fear)
he moves to step astraddle
now what will be, will surely be,
for the breaker's in the saddle.

Here we redefine commitment,
for it's now the horse's deal;
the breaker's foot is shoved
into the stirrup to the heel.

The ride might end with two as one,
just like it all began,
else the breaker finds the wherewithal
to rise and ride again.

With Triple-digit temperatures,
it's tough to hang and rattle,
the breaker's butt is heatsore
and bleeding in the saddle.

Hail the horses of the nations,
hear the stories of them told,
how they've carried kingdom's armies,
how they've won Olympic Gold.

Carried Washington and Paul Revere,
helped set our country free,
carried Roosevelt and Houston,
John Wayne, and Grant, and Lee.

One thing they have in common,
their stories all begin
with one you seldom hear about—
the breaker in the pen.

THE SHADOW ON THE CUTBANK

History wrote his epitaph
When barbed-wire cut the range,
While he was but an embryo
Adjusting to the change,

But he was not aborted
By the creaking stretch of wire
And the numbers still are legion
Of the horseback man for hire.

His shadow cast at sunrise
On a cutbank wall of sand
Is a mate to some conquistador's
In Coronado's band.

He is steeped in the traditions
Of those horsemen long ago.
He is rumored to be mortal
Though he won't admit it's so.

Since the glory that was Camelot
With her dragons breathing fire,
The hero of the world has been
The horseback man for hire.

His glory days aren't over
In spite of all we've read
He is no less than he ever was
No matter what's been said.

In the deserts of the hi-tech world
He's trailing up his cattle
He will never quit his horses
And he'll never sell his saddle.

THE MEN WHO RIDE NO MORE

"Bronc to Breakfast" calendars hang fading on the walls
There's a lost and aimless wandering through corridors and halls
Of slippered feet that shuffle on a waxed and polished floor
And vacant stares of emptiness from men who ride no more

Men who once rode proudly—men with long straight backs
Men who covered hill and plain with steel shod horses tracks
Now pass their idle days in rooms with numbers on the door
With orderlies and nurses for the men who ride no more

Time was when spur rowels jingled when boot heels bumped the floor
Dawns with hot black coffee and saddling up at four
With feet in tapaderos and broncs between their knees
And silken neck scarves snapping as they turned into the breeze

From full-blown living legends true to riding for the brand
To the scarcely mediocre who could hardly make a hand
They would gather for the branding or the shipping in the Fall
Now it's walker, cane, and wheelchair in the antiseptic hall

And they all have their mementos on the table by their side
Like a cracked and fading snapshot of a horse they usta ride
Or standing with the wife beside a thirty-seven Ford
A high-heeled boot hooked nonchalant on a muddy running board

Just instants frozen from the past that somehow give a clue
To who and what they were before their riding days were through
Horseback men with horseback rules from horseback days of yore
Their one and only wish would be to somehow ride once more

To once more rope a soggy calf and drag it to the fire
To long-trot for a half a day and see no post or wire
To ride a morning circle—catch a fresh one out at noon
And trot him in when day was done to the rising of a moon

To put in one more horseback day and have just one more chance
To ride home to a pretty wife and drive her to a dance
To take her hand and hold her close and waltz across a floor
Before the time to join the ranks of men who ride no more.

SHADY VALLEYS

The horseman was a soldier
Word had it—none was bolder
Hence; the orders in the folder
    Sent him with the Light Brigade
In the ghastly scene that followed
Was the gallant unit swallowed
Where in bloody grass they wallowed
    There in the valley shade
Then the lucky who were spared
Rode back where no one cared
Determined shoulders squared
    And somewhat wiser now
These descendants of the knighted
Who in their quests delighted
At the wrongs that they had righted
    Yet it seemed a waste somehow
One would deem it somewhat strange
That in all of hist'ry's range
There is noted little change
    When sounds the battle call and
Fighting gallantly as told
At the urging of the old
The youthful and the bold
    Become names upon the wall.

SONG OF THE PACKER

Down from the peaks and pinnacles,
And up from the canyon floor,
Through passes and fountains of immature mountains
Where big-hearted rivers roar

Comes a sound that is mostly imagined
By the wildest stretch of the mind,
Only to blast out from some promontory
Like ten philharmonics combined.

Can you hear? It's the song of the packer —
The ballad of man, horse and mule
Who gamble on hands dealt by nature
Where earth and the elements rule.

It's a song of the mountains and timber,
And it's mainly a song of the West
From the man who still cargoes the sawbuck and Decker
The man, some say, hasn't progressed.

He's sold his soul to the mountains,
Though a good woman might own his heart,
And the two-diamond hitch that he throws on his canvas
Has the touch of Rembrandt's art.

And though his vocabulary
Rivals those of the sea and the sail
He explains that his colorful language
Helps line out his mules on the trail.

But he's motherhood soft on the inside
And his very core feels a thrill
At the vapor that blows from the throat of an elk
As it bugles from some frosty hill.

Just look at the sling ropes and crowsfeet
And the picket line froze hard as sin
See the axe on the side of the lead mule's pack
Cause the trail is prob'ly blowed-in.

See the product of evolution
Culmination of savvy and brawn
A legacy passed down from Genghis Khan's army
The packers of history's dawn.

Hear the music transcending the continents
And breeds and races and time.
The mountain man's national anthem
Is heard in the clank and the chime

Of the bells as they sway in the moonlight
On the necks of the trail-weary string—
In the raven's call—in the eagle's scream
And the metered rowel's ring.

The tempo is set to the seasons,
To the weather and Geography,
Or the whim of an unpredictable mule,
And it's "classical music" to me.

FAMILY FENCES

a family fixes fences
moves from post to post
mending

I walk ahead, lean into diamond willow
posts slowly rotting
pull staples out, undo wire

our son follows
his eye on the line,
the next horizon
he sets new posts in place

his child runs back and forth
carries staples
learns the place where the sagehen nests
where the coyote makes its den and which
cry is the ferruginous hawk
which the prairie falcon
learns the names of flowers
                    shooting star and buffalo bean
absorbs the scent of wolf willow

and you, coming behind
you staple old wire to new posts

each spring this is the way
a family fences

BREAKING POETS

how do we keep the poets
out of the corrals
always is a poem snubbed to a post
jerking back, snapping rope
about the time we're ready to
throw the saddle on
and buck 'em out the gate

it's a lousy way to make a living
breaking poets
poets returning to the corrals
for another horse and another

HELLFIRE

that's where LA cattle were branded
when I was a child

my father
one or two of my brothers
a hired man
rode in from the north,
others came from the camp
circled, came in from the west
bunched the cattle as they came

branding day
I hung on the top rail
lined up empty vaccine bottles
too little to help
just big enough to get in the pictures

the last LA cattle
were branded in the same corrals
I sat on the top rail again
waited, knowing my turn would come too soon

I clenched the LA irons
pressed the irons against the calf's hide
my eyes blurred, the sting of smoke
and regret
my father's knife in one hand
the calf's sack in the other
one swipe of the blade
I held testicles,
pulled each one down
scraped the cords
the same way I saw my father do it
hundreds and hundreds of times

no one said a word

ANTHEM

And in the morning I was riding
Out through the breaks of that long plain,
And leather creaking in the quieting
Would sound with trot and trot again.
I lived in time with horse hoof falling;
I listened well and heard the calling
The earth, my mother, bade to me,
Though I would still ride wild and free.
And as I flew out on the morning,
Before the bird, before the dawn,
My heart would beat the world a warning —
Those horsemen now rode all with me,
And we were good, and we were free.

We were not told, but ours the knowing
We were the native strangers there
Among the things the land was growing —
To know this gave us more the care
To let the grass keep at its growing,
To let the streams keep at their flowing.
We knew the land would not be ours,
That no one has the awful pow'rs
To claim the vast and common nesting,
To own the life that gave him birth,
Much less to rape his mother earth
And ask her for a mother's blessing,
And ever live in peace with her,
And, dying, come to rest with her.

Oh, we would ride and we would listen
And hear the message on the wind.
The grass in morning dew would glisten
Until the sun would dry and blend
The grass to ground and air to skying.
We'd know by bird or insect flying,

Or by their mood or by their song,
If time and moon were right or wrong
For fitting works and rounds to weather.
The critter coats and leaves of trees
Might flash some signal with a breeze —
Or wind and sun on flow'r or feather.
We knew our way from dawn to dawn,
And far beyond, and far beyond.

It was the old ones with me riding
Out through the fog fall of the dawn,
And they would press me to deciding
If we were right or we were wrong.
For time came we were punching cattle
For men who knew not spur nor saddle,
Who came with locusts in their purse
To scatter loose upon the earth.
The savage had not found this prairie
Til some who hired us came this way
To make the grasses pay and pay
For some raw greed no wise or wary
Regard for grass could satisfy.
The old ones wept, and so did I.

Do you remember? We'd come jogging
To town with jingle in our jeans,
And in the wild night we'd be bogging
Up to our hats in last month's dreams.
It seemed the night could barely hold us
With all those spirits to embold' us
While, horses waiting on three legs,
We'd drain the night down to the dregs.
And just before beyond redemption
We'd gather back to what we were.
We'd leave the money left us there
And head our horses for the wagon.
But in the ruckus, in the whirl,
We were the wolves of all the world.

The grass was growing scarce for grazing,
Would soon turn sod or soon turn bare.
The money men set to replacing
The good and true in spirit there.
We could not say, there was no knowing,
How ill the future winds were blowing.
Some cowboys even shunned the ways
Of cowboys in the trail herd days
(But where's the gift not turned for plunder?),
Forgot that we are what we do
And not the stuff we lay claim to.
I dream the spell that we were under;
I throw in with a cowboy band
And go out horseback through the land.

So mornings now I'll go out riding
Through pastures of my solemn plain,
And leather creaking in the quieting
Will sound with trot and trot again.
I'll live in time with horse hoof falling;
I'll listen well and hear the calling
The earth, my mother, bids to me,
Though I will still ride wild and free.
And as I ride out on the morning
Before the bird, before the dawn,
I'll be this poem, I'll be this song.
My heart will beat the world a warning —
Those horsemen will ride all with me,
And we'll be good, and we'll be free.

BUM THINKING NOWHERE NEAR A HORSE

If you see me sittin' sorrowful, all busted and stove-up
And you wonder how a puncher gits that way,
I can tell you at the start-off to avoid all work aground
If you rope and ride ahorseback for yore pay.

It's all right to shoe your horses and to braid and mend yore tack,
All that work aground that keeps you in the saddle.
But yore mind gits misdirected if you try yore hand at chores
Beneath stomping out the broncs and punchin' cattle.

Now and then old Majordomo, he'd come roust me during slack
And suggest I patch his roof or plow his garden,
Or do some posthole diggin' or go scale some tall windmills,
But I'd always tell 'im, "Please, I begs yore pardon."

But it so happened that one Sunday I was early in from town
And was holdin' down the bunkhouse all alone
When the boss, he done convinces me that if I'd pull one chore,
Tackin' hack hooves next day would be quicker done.

"All them shoes are in a whiskey barrel up in the barn hayloft,
Standing right beside that hayloft pulley door.
Though it took us five to hoist 'em up, I figures comin' down
All that gravity is worth them four men more."

Wal, I'm nowhere near a horse, so it makes good sense to me.
I go don my chaps and spurs and gits my rope,
Then I ambles to the barn and up the ladder to the loft,
Thinkin' I can git this job done in a lope.

So I straps a big old jug knot tie around that whiskey barrel,
Runs the rope out through the pulley to the ground.
Then I delicately balances that barrel on the edge,
And I rushes out to gently let 'er down.

Well, I runs the rope around my tail and takes a hitch in front
To control the downward progress of the barrel.

Then I gives the jerk that tilts the barrel out of that hayloft door —
And that's the insult that begins our little quarrel.

See, that barrel of horseshoes had to weigh a good four hundred pounds,
More than twice what I would weigh all wet and dressed.
So when I tell you that my rope hitch HITCHED and slipped up underarm,
Then I figure you can guess most of the rest.

I plumb parts with earth quite suddenly, ablastin' for the sky,
But I meets that barrel 'bout halfway up that barn.
This wreck, it slows my progress some, but it ain't slowed for long
'Fore I'm headin' for that pulley and yardarm.

When that barrel hits the bottom and my pore head hits the top
And it rings that pulley like a midway gong
Where those fellers swing the hammers for to show off with the girls —
Wal, you might think that it's over . . . But you're wrong.

See, the crashin' of that old stave barrel all weighed down with that steel
Caused the bottom to bust out and dump its load,
So I'm plummeting from heaven now about the speed of sound,
And I'm speedin' on a dang'rous deadend road.

But that devil barrel, it slaps me blind and sideways one more time
As it flies up and I'm acrashin' down.
THEN you'd think this stubborn accident would be about played out
When I breaks a few more bones upon the ground.

No. The rope goes slack. The hitch unhitches. I lie gazin' up.
Then I close my eyes and gives me up for dead.
'Cause the last thing that I see before I wakes, all splinted up,
Is that cussed barrel acomin' fer my head.

NOTES FOR A NOVEL

"I cannot sleep. All time is passing.
The old days fade like dusking light.
Oh, fast awake, I want a sounding
That carried sleep one long gone night."

    Uneasy on his bunking
    Snubbed up fast against the window
    He starts another tossing ride he hopes
    Will go to sleep.
    He counts the marks and circumstance
    On day rounds back there ridden.
    This is a journey lasting long
    That seldom comes complete.

"Young with breezes blowing round me,
Ride I'd ride the lightlong day.
Then lay me down. My day deserved it.
How sound I'd sleep the night away."

    The science sounds
    Out of crowd and combustion
    The smell of cloisture no pastoral priest
    No native nun with prairie vows
    Would put up with—
    Not in the least.

"So dream, I'll dream of cowcamp days
Where noisiness was cricket calls . . . . "
This was the night it came to him—
The windmill sounding tugs and falls.

II

"His wife says Sweeney never sleeps,
Lies there gasping wide-eyed like a grounded fish.
No nightmare growls, just dog peeps.
I went over and talked to him.
Roundabout he made a wish."

　　　His bit shank broke on one high dive
　　　The bronc he fanned took through the dawn.
　　　He'd come undone. The next good heave
　　　Unloaded him. He landed wrong.

"He comes up with words.
Reads now like a monastery monk.
Far away like and feeling punk
He goes talking about an urge —
Or he might be just plain drunk —
The nights he says are not right anymore —
An urge to buy a windmill for . . .
For its tintinnabulation
The gentle measured stroke
Bringing forth juices
The quiet clamor and secret exclamation . . ."

　　　They'd saddle-sleighed him from the breaks,
　　　A rope and blanket travois sling.
　　　He saw him dying in their eyes —
　　　But fluttered there no angel wing . . .

"He read, though, even then.
Those two books in his saddlebag
That day we brought him in.
He lay there limp like a rag
So sort of unalive.
We turned him over. All we saw there living
Was his eyes."

He knew one thought would make him live
If he would get the thought down right.
So through the pain and through the shock
Of body gone he thought of light.

"He grinned. It kind of calmed us down.
It had looked bad. We were afraid.
It took awhile to make a sound.
Catch the horse, he said.
Cinnamon, remember? The counterfeit son-of-a-bitch."

October moon and dawn comingled
Light of morning short of sun
The sun was still outside the morning
Light of dawn was not yet done.

"Ten minutes before we thought
By now he might be dead.
But there he was instead
Saying to build that sledding cot
With his saddle blanket and rope.
We brought him slow up out of there."

The dawn's light brightens night's innocent air;
The full sun crystals, makes course the day;
The sun heats hard, the light sweeps bare:
This was his thought as they bore him away.

III

The cattle foraged up the plain
Within a walk of surface streams,
So tablelands of pristine grass
Were only grazed in ranchers' dreams.

Grass, grass, stretching for stirrup high,
Golden flowing waves licked by the wind
Miles wherever you looked.
The cliché holds—a sea of grass.

Then someone spired the bladed mill
Atop a tower to reach the wind
And pump the water, spread the range
And speculator's dividend.

Came the grind of gear and metal.
How it grated,
Began the lowly chores aground
That slowly brought the cowboy down.
He had said hiring out
I'm a roper and rider and wild hoss fighter.
Now he'd shuffle, add the tout
. . . And a pretty good windmill climber.

What gave the range took it away.
The plowman came in the windmill's wake
And towed behind a grasping thirst
The well on well would never slake.

IV

In halfsleep came the cymbal clang . . . no, clamor of an Asian gong
    In echo from a canyon in the breakland down the plain,
But it followed on the slightest exclamation that the metal makes
    As windmills reach their pumping cycle's peak and coast again.

What could this mean? He comes awake, lies wide-eyed in the darkness
    And sees the boy in quilts gone sleepy to the sounding air.
He pillows his head to hide the blush brought on by this rude meaning.
    He struggles up and paces through the room in his wheelchair.

He brakes the wheeled contraption by the back door, stops to listen,
    Stops to listen to the wheeling sound of breezes sliced by blades.
The cycle sound comes back to him — the rods ringing their casing,
    Far below the watered rattling of the brass ball in its cage.

What cage is this around him now that goes on wheels of metal,
    Around this Luddite cowboy mad his cinchring was of steel,
Who labored long to shape some bits and spurs of twisted rawhide,
    Who thought he'd slept by prairie sound but rested to the mill?

To pass the time, to prop his pride he'd metaphored his standing
    Through books he read, mythologized the race he'd so far run.
Now Icarus ahorseback, flown the labyrinth of common life,
    He'd in his exultation circled too close to the sun.

Or had he been Bellerophontes on the winged Pegasus
    And in his labors proved so good he'd thought to ride with gods
Who punished his rude impudence by feeding him his soul
    Away from horses, banned from grass, fighting urban odds?

V

Was their pard holed up there
Feelin' sorry for hisself?

And it came to pass
The pardners of cowboy Sweeney's recent days
Palavered around a table at a creekside camp
For they had ridden together
As princes of the Earth and if they could
They would allay his sorrow.
He did not rest well in town
He did not rest well at all
And dear patient Miz S wondered
If life went so limp for all the punchers
Whose spurs were on the peg.

So drunk sometimes he could not
Hit the floor with his hat
His stories sometimes took a different turn . . . .
Picture this: At the county fair carnival
There is a Sideshow for Cynics Only
Featuring a Quartet of Luddites
In Wheelchairs singing
        We'd argue till the cows come home
        But we've no longer a leg to stand on . . . .

He's all bent out of shape
Now that he's figured out his sleep
Came to that old prairie lullaby
Of a windmill's sounding beat
And he hated climbing the infernal contraptions
Worse than any of them.
He had finally said
I guess if you need an iron lung
You need an iron lung

And if you need a windmill . . . well . . .
(And too he had thought those penetrations
Nuisances like mosquito bites
But did not the mill keep up
Its affectionate stroking of the earth
In the wildest of weather
While he cursed the wind
And was he no less a stranger than the mill?)

The wife went from the room slamming doors
Not only the cost but an eyesore
And what woman wants a windmill
Pumping away in the fecund garden spot
Of her private place?

> One opening is all they needed
> To take out a loan
> And plan a big party benefit
> And it came on the key word "operate" —
> The hitch was the ordinance
> Against using the thing in town
> But didn't say anything about its erection.

Yes, and let it stroke one sucker rod deep
In a well-wetted vessel
Just for the sound coming with it.
Strange the wife objected like that
Till later when the urgency
The gist of the matter
Sunk in on her.

VI

A band of cowboys learned their pardner Sweeney couldn't sleep
    unless he heard the pumping of a windmill.
Not only was this problem foreign to their expertise,
    they also had to keep it confidential.

For Sweeney—stove up two years now and grounded in the town—
    though sore bereft of jingle in the pockets
(He'd hocked down to three saddles, chaps, eight bridled bits with reins,
    four horsehair belts, five hats, three sets of sprockets)

Would ruffle like a hen and shunt aside the proffered boost
    with awkward pride he'd one day leave behind,
And all their wives, the neighbors, bureaucrats at City Hall,
    informed could put their project in a bind.

They found an eight-foot Aereo with a twenty-four foot tower
    unerected by a bankrupt farmer's barn.
They threw their party, got a loan, and pieced the mill to town.
    The drilling rig set off the big alarm.

There's much more to the story than you'll find here in these notes:
    neighbor pickets, civil suits, two divorces.
But the mill was raised to breezes and its cycle set to sound,
    And Sweeney had good nights and dreamed of horses.

And it was horses he was riding, he was riding in the wind
(The windmill wheels and whirs and clangs so lightly in the wind)
    And when he rode men might his rowels hear
    Jingling in a whistling wind so clear.

And now at last a maid he's won; he takes her in his arms—
There's timing to his resting now and rhythm to his charms.
    His barren places now are watered bright,
    And he's a varry, parfit, gentile knight.

CHILD OF THE PLAINS

I write from trees and mountain rocks,
There aren't too many on your plain.
I think of you and think of grass
That covers place and place again.

These trees stretch up to soothe the sight
From seeing far too much too far,
As if we could not stand beside
The length we look up to a star.

Well, you and I, we cast our loops
And trees will tangle up our throw,
And what we catch or might not catch
Will take us time and time to know.

The trees, like pictures on old walls,
Hide fades and scars and what's behind,
But I'd as soon your blades of grass
Were underneath, we are its kind.

SONGDOG

When young I saw a coyote spring in air
And arc and tumble in a backward flip,
Then chase his tail and wallow in his joy,
Exalting with his private yap and yip.

Caught up, I sprang from hiding to my horse
And somersaulted backward to the ground,
Then rolled and wallowed in the flow'rs and grass
And mocked the private rapture of his sound.

And not a few times horseback in the breaks
The arcane wiliness the songdogs store
Behind those yellow and enigmatic eyes
Had punctured pride and schooled me in the lore.

Perhaps you've watched a coyote watching you
With all the unconcern you'd watch a bird
Guarding with ruffled threats its pasture nest,
Yes, watching as your mind and fingers stirred

A strategy to line him on the run
And uncoil just one loop one time and bunch
Yourself in with that rarest horseback crowd
Who claim in truth they roped a coyote once.

The facing bluffs that rose above the draw
Were rock along their rims. On one sat I
Ahorseback, watching him across the way.
A touch of steel and I was on the fly

Across the bluff to line him out along
The plain, but when I reached the farther rim
Where nonchalantly he had looked at me,
I looked from where I came and looked at him

So nonchalantly watching me. And now
I think in marrow-bone and not in mind
Of times a thousand sleeps ago and more
And hope he figured I was worth his time.

It's told in myth he made the grassy range,
Perhaps some dusk in an expansive mood.
Coyote was never careful with his work,
So it turned out even parts of ill and good.

He haired the drying crust after the flood,
Then people of the grass grew tribe by tribe
From feathers of his many-colored prey
He saved to plant after the flood had dried.

The winking and disheveled stars he tricked
Out of their ordered ranks for making wars
As troublesome in heavens as on earth,
And made Miss Venus brighter'n Mister Mars.

He's choice and chance, yin and yang, he's known
No more for his exploits than for his famous mistakes.
But, right or wrong, I'll guess how this will end will end:
With that last song he sings out in the breaks.

But meantime, Coyote, save a song for me,
For that first night I'm gone, late or soon,
And add it to that banquet of your sound
You spread for setting sun and rising moon?

I would not pay to die, make maggot mulch.
I'd have a jolly band of horseback friends
Come pack this flesh and bone toward your songdog feast
In the grass by a pot-bellied moon where some mesa ends.

The corrupted flesh of man's not to your taste,
But, Coyote, clean this flesh from all this bone
And turn it into grass that turns to flesh
And leave me rendered, quiet, and quite alone.

A PONDER

And was I real or was I dreaming?
Was I that boy, "so good of face"?
Were we so good, or are we scheming
To forge a role that garners grace?
We rode our horses 'cross the grasses
In flight from Babel's huddled masses.
We were the offside of the coin;
We didn't care to court or join
The mad pursuit of pelf or puissance;
We left our money on the bar —
A crude disdain, perhaps, but far
Contrary to the crass insistence
On hierarchy's servility
That passes for civility.

We didn't spend much time defining
Our role, but were we to define:
"To do what's right with careful timing,
To be the right place the right time,"
Would pretty well sum up our duties.
We learned by look and feel, not studies —
Unless it was the moves of pards
Ahorseback, eloquent as bards.
It was a spark and we would fan it
While riding favored by good winds
With favored ancients, proper ends.
The owners merely mined the granite;
We were the sculptors of the herd.
Yes, ours the poetry, theirs the word.

The Goddess handed me the bridle
That tamed my horse's summer heart.
Then, by the spring and standing idle,
He took my saddle, took his part
In works of rounds I would be keeping.
In consecrating moonlight meeting

I joined myself to Mother Earth
And put in order first things first.
I pledged my heart; I made my promise
To love her faithfully till death
Despite enigmas, even with
The burdens of those moods that harm us.
I joined to her in mortal cord
To tender thought and work and word.

We toil so hard by sun, we're abler
By light of moon to know our part.
So things that I would take from labor
I'd carry only in my heart.
The death millenniums behind me,
Lift up the stone and you will find me.
The true man dwelling in the dream,
I listen and remember when
Each thing was sung into existence
And carried yet its proper name.
The Moon might bring that time again
If it can calm the Sun's resistance.
Beyond the din of dusty day
There is no closed place I must stay.

When thought is clear, things fall in place,
We'll grasp the mood of Nature's face,
We'll know the texture of real grace.

SEASON SONG

If I'd go back
Then back I'd go
On caroled air
On season snow.

The churches chime
A season song
To toll our time
Too fast along.

We stroll downtown
All up and down
All up and down
All season long
All wrapped in song.

MY PONY

Coming back to you, my pony, whom I had to leave
To make money, I proffer up the dire smidgen,
The torn thing I managed to lug back with me,

Along with the big bucks: World is made of bologna.
Like the pressed woods of my ascetic bookcase,
Like the traffic jam full of air conditioning

And grieving music, world is pressed together
As if my impossibility, my pony, as by poetry . . . .
How long I have loved thee to see you now grown old

Though still able — under all this weight —
To put your foot to the far off, to the going . . . .
Carry me now, my pony. Carry us to where we buried

Those Clydesdales who once in soggy spring,
In early morning, plowed those furrows which fed us
Before I could no longer afford the farm.

I think we laid them down, me scrounging money
For the backhoe, over there in the west field.
I think we should go over now to the west field . . . .

And the cats who used to run with us back
In the olde days: Sartre, Huck, and the others —
None lived to see fourteen, though all stayed relatively

Long for cat lives — blessings to them now, my pony;
Blessings to them who used to run and sit with us!
And will I ever get to hold my father as he dies

And will he release me then from the fear of dying?
Not likely. Probably not, my pony.
Probably much more mulling through this membrane

Which passes so quickly, which stuns me and makes me
Wonder how much longer we've both got here to ride . . . .
Ride on while we're here, my pony, and next spring

I'll bring Virginia, whom I've left back in the city.
I'll bring her to you for her safekeeping.
She needs the hurl and arc these fields have put in us,

Out looking; she needs the kind of joking past grieving
We've come to together, thrown through the pressed world
Where I went off to earn being hers and yours, your Liam.

SAYS HARRY
—for Harry Jackson and Don Champlin

Don, huge of heart and girth, and I
dropped by to Harry's place
in Cody on a rain-warm day
in spring, Hart Mountain's postcard face
alight, late afternoon.

We came to see the art, to pay
respects. "My lawyer's here,"
says Harry, settling in a chair,
"no time to visit now,"
while pointing out, hung in a frame,

some New York City mobster saints
he'd neighbored in his early days.
"I never locked my doors,"
says Harry, as our trail-herd talk
began to scatter, no one riding swing

as lawyers know on Harry's drives
they ride the drags so, for an hour,
more or less, we gathered strays. Says Harry,
"Shake a loop out" and we did, for catch-colt
Buster George, foundling prince of Lambshead spread;

for young Marines; for whores
across the Rio Grande; for Texas Rangers'
locked-and-cocked engraved, pearl-handled forty-fives;
for Charlie Goodnight, and for ev'ry old
cowpuncher still at work.

We kept on ropin', punchin' holes
in twines of twisted threads
from story yarns, each half-begun
before the next broke from the herd.
Says Harry, "We could drink all night

these whiskey words and not get drunk"
as we went reeling out the door
to Texas and to Italy.
Says Harry, "Come back!" And we will,
to see the art, to pay respects.

BENEDICTION AFTER A GATHERING OF COWBOY POETS

It's night in Nara Visa, perfect black,
September waxing moon, an equal white,
no shades of gray between them in the light
that boils out of the windows in the back
behind the kitchen counter. It is gold,
and pools like lava out into the night
to puddle in the parking lot in bright
translucent patches on the dust. An old
melodic fiddle tune escapes in sharp
staccato batches from the dance-hall, slight
as red and orange leaves in scattered flight
upon a staggered wind. Within this warp
of time and space, I nurse a plastic cup
of warm tequila, vapors coiled-up tight
around my head, its sweet primeval bite
upon my lip, my aching tongue curled-up,
vibrating like a snake's. I'll taste it yet
with you, this hum of poetry; the trite
and clumsy, helpless passages I write
they will be brilliant gems you'll not forget,
they'll burn the miles between us like the names
of every passion, every appetite
and all the incantations that ignite
in cool New Mexico my heart to flames.

THE STUMP-GRUBBERS

No tree can live forever. When one dies,
it dies in leaf and bud and bit by bit
and limb by limb by limb, until it dries
in heart and root, and naught remains of it

but stump, where once its open branches spread.
We throw a chain around the trunk and hitch
our Belgians or our Percherons to sled
and grub it out and drag it clear and pitch

the deadfall and the smaller stuff on top,
then strike the fire to feel its ashen breath
and listen to the nervous crack and pop
of new life stirring in the last of death.

THE RED-TAIL HAWK

I know what lifts the red-tail hawk,
What pumps the thunderstorm,
What snaps the thistle at its stalk,
And how the hoo-doos form;

I know what whips the playa lake,
What spins the windmill fan,
What dunes the dust, what drifts the flake,
And how the howl began;

I know what gathers up to blow
What gives the grass to bend —
I know these things, yet I'll not know
What reason has of wind.

I know what whirls and dances me,
What fancy turns my eye,
What little things add up to be,
And how the soul can fly;

I know what in me wants the touch,
What aches in the embrace,
What excess never is too much,
And how to measure grace;

I know what gathers up to show
What fragile stuff we're of —
I know these things, yet I'll not know
What reason has of love.

Of wind or love, what reason has
I will not ever know —
Not why, not whether, not whereas;
Yet where they go, I go.

WHEN THE DEVIL PLAYS
HIS FIDDLE

The tank's gone dry,
The grass is brittle,
The sand in the wind
Stings like grease from the griddle;
If it rained all day —
Too late, too little —
There's Hell to pay
When the Devil plays his fiddle.
There's Hell to pay
When the Devil plays his fiddle.

Went to the bank,
They were non-committal
But I could not beg
For the money to feed my cattle.
Curse or pray
Or stick to the middle —
There's Hell to pay
When the Devil plays his fiddle.
There's Hell to pay
When the Devil plays his fiddle.

When the dust and sand
Are rosin in his hands
The high-line sings
Like a loose bow scrapin' on the strings.

Goin' dead broke
Makes my remittal;
He carves my soul
While the good men spit and whittle.
Come what may,
Come a damn fool riddle —
There's Hell to pay
When the Devil plays his fiddle.
There's Hell to pay
When the Devil plays his fiddle.

ASHES, AFTER FIRE

I've seen the bluestem, stirrup-deep,
Become a blackened pyre,
A wasteland, buried in the heap
Of ashes, after fire.

The old, dead grass goes up in smoke,
The wind howls in the wire,
What was, is gone, deep in the cloak
Of ashes, after fire.

Yet quick, so quick, the ranges wear
Their spanking new attire,
As tender grass grows in the care
Of ashes, after fire.

Though alchemists have lost their call
Their magics still inspire
Gold seekers in the grimy pall
Of ashes, after fire.

A PRAIRIE MOTHER'S PRAYER

He's so small,
Such a tiny thing;
He needs my all,
He needs everything that is dear
In a mother's care,
So, god, please hear his prairie mother's prayer:

> Let him bend
> Before the wind,
> Lift him up
> When he's laid low,
> Let a thunderstorm
> His spirit form,
> Fill his cup
> With rain and snow,
> Let him green his days
> As seasons pass,
> Let him grow I pray
> The way of the grass.

At my breast,
He is innocence;
His life is blessed
With the sacred sense of the gift,
And there's none so fair
As a baby with his prairie mother's prayer.

> Let him bend
> Before the wind,
> Lift him up
> When he's laid low,
> Let a thunderstorm
> His spirit form,
> Fill his cup
> With rain and snow,

Let him green his days
As seasons pass,
Let him grow I pray
The way of the grass.

Fathers pray
That their sons grow strong,
Come what may,
Come to right or wrong; mothers live
What their babies bear
And so I give this prairie mother's prayer:

Let him bend
Before the wind,
Lift him up
When he's laid low,
Let a thunderstorm
His spirit form,
Fill his cup
With rain and snow,
Let him green his days
As seasons pass,
Let him grow I pray
The way of the grass.

BUCK

The December my horse died, I did not
go to midnight mass
to celebrate with a single sip of wine
Christ's birth. Instead, lit
between a nimbus moon and new snow,
I guzzled mezcal and mimicked the caroling
coyotes down the crick
where weeks earlier I dragged Buck
behind the pickup—horizontal
hooves at an awkward trot
in the side mirror, an image
I'll take with me to hell. No backhoe,
no D-8 Cat to dig a grave with, I left
him in deep bunchgrass, saffron
belly toward the south
like a warm porch light thrown
suddenly over those singing
No-el, No-el . . . .
                      Riding the same ground
that past spring for horned cow skulls
to adorn our gates, I spotted four
bleached white as puffballs,
methodically stuffed them
into a *never-tear* trash bag,
balanced the booty
off one thigh and tried to hold
jog-trot Buck to a walk,
my forefinger hefting
the left rein to curb
his starboard glance.
                      One by one,
like spook-show aliens hatching
from human brisket, white shoots popped
through that hot black plastic
gleaming in noon sun that turned
my grasp to butterfat. And when I reached,

lifting to retwist my grip,
it was sputnik flying low, it was
Satan's own crustacean unleashed, it was *the*
prehistoric, eight-horned, horse-eating bug
that caught Buck's eye
the instant his lit fuse hit powder. Lord,
how that old fat pony, living
up to his name one last time,
flashed his navel at angels,
rattled and rolled my skulls like dice,
and left me on all fours
as he did on that Christmas—high-
lonesomed, hurt, and howling
not one holy word toward the bones.

ALL THIS WAY FOR THE SHORT RIDE

—In Memory of Joe Lear

After grand entry cavalcade of flags,
Star-Spangled Banner, stagecoach figure 8s
in a jangle of singletrees, after trick riders
sequined in tights, clowns in loud getups,
queens sashed pink or chartreuse
in silk—after the fanfare—the domed
rodeo arena goes lights-out
black: stark silent
prayer for a cowboy crushed by a ton
of crossbred Brahma.
                              What went wrong—
too much heart behind a high kick,
both horns hooking earth, the bull vaulting
a half-somersault to its back—
each witness recounts with the same
gruesome note: the wife
stunned in a bleacher seat
and pregnant with their fourth. In this dark
behind the chutes, I strain to picture,
through the melee of win with loss,
details of a classic ride—body curled
fetal to the riggin', knees up,
every spur stroke in perfect sync,
chin tucked snug. In this dark,
I rub the thick neck of my bronc, his pulse
rampant in this sudden night
and lull. I know the instant
that bull's flanks tipped beyond
return, how the child inside
fought with his mother for air
and hope, his heart with hers
pumping in pandemonium—in shock,
how she maundered in the arena
to gather her husband's bullrope and hat, bells

clanking to the murmur of crowd
and siren's mewl.
                    The child learned early
through pain the amnion could not protect him from,
through capillaries of the placenta, the sheer
peril of living with a passion
that shatters all at once
from infinitesimal fractures
in time. It's impossible, when dust
settling to the backs of large animals
makes a racket you can't think in,
impossible to conceive that pure fear,
whether measured in degrees of cold
or heat, can both freeze
and incinerate so much
in mere seconds. When I nod
and they throw this gate open to the same
gravity, the same 8 ticks
of the clock, number 244 and I
will blow for better or worse
from this chute—flesh and destiny up
for grabs, a bride's bouquet
pitched blind.

TO WALLACE

—For Ruth, Clint, Allison & Natalie

I'm not applauding cathouse towns in Idaho,
nor rednecked gov'nors who reigned in Alabama.
The Wallace I tip my beaver lid to is my hero,
that Cowboy Poet Lariat—McRae—
from the Rocker Six, up Rosebud Crick, Montana.

I said *Cowboy Poet*, and those are two big words,
as tall and deep to fill as red-topped Paul Bond boots.
A Cowboy Poet cuts strong verses from the herds,
savvies cattle, horseflesh, grass, and water,
lives the history and tradition, loves their deepest roots.

And that fits Wallace, like his saddle, stem to stern—
land-loving navyman, cavvyman, pistolero poet.
And top-hand actor, too, they say, because he'll burn
and go for broke on that cowpoke hole card, heart—
Wallace packs the ace and he's damn proud to show it.

Which is why his five-gaited iambs move so true
with keen vision, image, spry rhythm, rhyme and wit.
The wise, old farrier hammering out a shoe,
Wallace loves that ballpeen-anvil chime
as he forges and he shapes each red-hot line to fit.

And how his flinty, roughstock eye can size-up folks—
between the slats, they earn his praise or wrath in verse.
From dancehall damsels to itinerant cowpokes,
his gavel's not as fast as Judge Roy Bean's,
but hanging from his gallows, made of words, is worse.

And hard—oh Lord—how he fought hard to save the land
from the greed-monger Kid Russell called *the booster*.
When they demanded coal, he showed the bastards sand—
the grit of Sitting Bull and Crazy Horse
and Gallo del Cielo, Zaragoza's dueling rooster.

Did he win? Let's just say he doesn't know defeat.
There lives within the words themselves intrinsic worth.
You bet your kack, his verse will last beyond the beat
and power of those generating plants —
a poem-ghost-rider-posse crusading for the earth.

Here's to Wallace. Hoist his tartan like a bardic flag.
Long may the lingo of his calling ride the Tongue.
Montana's Robert Burns hard-charging with a brag
like ol' Casey on a bronc, Wallace,
reppin' for the legendary, keeps the old West young.

THE MEANING OF INTIMACY

—For Verlena Orr and Georgia

Not reasoning, but romantic
prehistoric instinct
coaxes my whiskered cheek to the bristled
muzzle of a colt working long-stemmed timothy-brome
hay evenly inward. My heart beats brisk
time to the rhythm of grinding teeth
crunching tiny pipettes of perfume — sweet
breath and music piped through the pink
nostrils into February air, so still,
so microscopically cold, I see its molecules
misting leafy green. The simplest poetic gift,
if we listen close, sings to the most
primitive sound churning into vision. Graced,
late last night, I sat in the easy
breathing warmth of cottonwood burning
without the slightest wheeze,
not a single creaking from the fir-
pine joints of the 90-year-old house. In the whisper
and whiff of fresh pencil lead
pressed firmly into notebook pages
curling, I felt the cat
rest her chin against my wool-
stockinged toes — purring and purring
her aboriginal rhythms into the fur-
bearing nerves of my words.

HIP-COCKED BRONCS

Through gates pivoting like pinball flippers,
through mazeworks of alleyways
and cutting quick 90s
into the catchpens, snorty horses are sorted
early, before full-bore July 4th sun, already
white-hot as a cinch ring
in the campfire of an early cowhand
out gathering slicks. Wet saddle pads
pressed thin, our flat waistlines fold
over the top lodgepole pine rails. We lean to read
the line-up of branded hips
for numbers posted beside names
on the draw sheet, *8 a.m. slack*
nailed beneath the crow's-nest. The grandstand
writhes with fans rousing to nightmare
hangovers in hot nylon bags
beginning to steam sour
while the hip-cocked broncs—steeped in the sweet
grass incense of their own scent, a light
dew misting off their backs—loll in dreams
before our 8-second shifts. Maybe
they twitch for the winning
every bit as real as we do
behind the chutes, slashing with a whip-
crack of fringed batwings, and rowels ticking
as we pace off maniacal rides
wild in our minds. We nod our heads
determined to spur pretty and win
our gypsy way to the next pitchin',
to another arena's rank bucker and buzzer,
Klaxon, welcome whistle, bell sounding
today oddly reminiscent
of that ricochet blare off lockers
years back in high school halls

between classes. I think I savvy now,
finally, the secret meaning
echoed by your 8-line poem
failing me so often
Mister Cody Bill Carlos Williams:

So much depends   So much depends
upon   upon

a red wheel   a red roan
barrow   bronco

glazed with rain   named The Grim
water   Reaper

beside the white   beside the word
chickens   Zarzyski

PUTTING THE RODEO TRY INTO
COWBOY POETRY

—In memory of Buck Ramsey

Let's begin with the wildest landscape, space
inhabited by far more of them
than our own kind and, yes, we *are* talking
other hearts, other stars. Fall in love with all
that is new born—universe, seedling, dawn,
human, foal, calf. Love equally
the seasons, know each sky has meaning,
winter the big lonesomes, the endless
horizons our hopes sink beyond
once every minute, sometimes
seeming never to rise
again for air or light,
for life. Fall *madly* in love
with earth's fickle ways. Heed
hard the cosmos cues, the most
minuscule pulsings, subtle nods—no heavy-
handed tap or poke, nothing muscular,
no near-death truths revealed, no telephone
or siren screaming us out of sleep
at 3 a.m. Forget revelation.
Forgive religion. Let's believe instead in song
bird, or Pegasus, the only angels
we'll ever need. Erase for good
inspiration from our Random Bunk-
House Dictionaries, from our petty heads
and pretty ambitions. Poetry is not
the grace or blessing we pray for—Poetry
is the Goddess for whom
we croon. Sing and surely we shall see
how she loves our music in any key—
any color, any creed, any race, any breed. Rhyme
if the muse or mood moves us
to do so. Go slow. Walk

then trot, lope then rock, and roll
for even a split second, our souls in the middle
of the whole storming world
getting western, throwing a tizzy fit,
our horses come-uncorked, just
as we were beginning to seriously think
we could turn the stampeding
words into a calm
milling herd of steers?

BIZARZYSKI, MAD POET AND CARPENTER SAVANT,
FEEDS
THE
BIRDS

Unlikely that my poems will ever land in some *Norton Anthology of Orni-thology*, let alone *The Guinness Bird Book of World Bon Appétit Records*, I want all you Audubon paisanos to hear right now who's the first mad poet to ring-shank-spike a fat foot-long freezer-burned muledeer salami to the icy top of a railroad tie corner post where I distract the rambunctious

flocks of ravenous magpies squawking happily all winter away from the purple finch—English sparrow birdseed feeders. Maybe I'm first also to have learned that even a scavenger clings to certain proprieties and will exercise its right to decline a handout. Once, I placed a frozen block of tofu atop the very same post. No way. Not one minuscule peck. Like offering menudo, paté, haggis to a vegan. Poor tofu—it didn't even get a second look, a quizzical magpie glance of comical disgust or surprise. I did not know these birds could smell, let alone whiff tofu at 30 below. I've watched them gobble-up a bloated road-killed polecat for brunch under a blacktop-softening sun. And so it sat there through five chinooks, through spring and summer, until the post, I sup-pose, osmosis-ed it (almost) along with that dan-gerous duo of dago hitmen, Sal Monella and his sidekick, Bocci, who must've thunk they'd bag a bird or two. But nothing bit the dust, just like nothing bit the tofu. And so now I must con-fess—because I'm catholic and I'm unfulfilled unless I'm bearing guilt—that I pray very hard for scavenger forgiveness, as they lay their beady eyes upon this latest feast and spiel: *My name is Paul. I'll be your server this winter. For your delight, our hammered chef tonight has spiked, in lieu of our usual alder-planked smoked salmon on the menu, fro-zen chunk of venison sopressa on creosoted post. It's free. I'll be right back to take your order.*

ONE SWEET EVENING JUST THIS YEAR

—For Ralph Beer and Wallace McRae

Sundown rolling up its softest nap
of autumn light over the foothills, grass
bales stacked two tiers above the '68 Ford's cab,
our long-toothed shadow slices east,
mudflaps dragging dry gumbo ruts
back home after one beer
at the Buckhorn Bar quenched the best
thirst I've worked-up
all millennium, pool balls clacking above the solemn
cowmen reminiscing their scripture,
waxing poetic lines to THE LEGEND
OF BOASTFUL BILL—*one sweet morning
long ago,* the hand-down favorite. I'll bet
this whole load, that old bard
Charles Badger Clark knew the eternal
bent of those words
the instant he scratched them across the open
range of the blank page.
                              Glacial melt
runneling over mountain rock,
moist air swirls in the cab
stirring up three decades of Montana
essences atomized
into a single mist—horse-cow-dog-drought
gunpowder-leather-runoff-grit-sage-sweat-
smoke-loss-whiskey-romance-song, all
tinctured by landscape and way of life
into a rural fragrance impossible to bottle—
these essences settling upon the porous
inner wrist of dusk
unfolding for only a moment
its sweet, unique blossom.
                              And me, tonight
I'm the lucky one along for the ride,
head still sweaty beneath my cap,
a harlequin glitter of hayseed
sticking to my bare arm stretched straight
out the window for no good reason

but to know my own pores rising beneath hair pressed flat
and flowing like grass in crick-bend shallows,
timothy in the side mirror, stems hanging on
with one arm and waving
wild with the other—to saffron yellow meadows
and rolling prairie flecked with cattle,
antelope, jackrabbit, grouse,
all grazing beneath one big gray
kite of bunched starlings'
acrobatic flashings over stubble.
                              We mosey home,
me and the old truck, in love
with our jag of good Montana grass—
not one speck of simplistic myth
between us and the west that was, sometimes
still is, and thus will be
forever and ever, amen.

POETRY IN MEMOIR

DEWCLAW

: a vestigial claw or hoof on the foot of certain mammals,
(because it reaches only the dewey surface of the ground).
                                    American Heritage Dictionary

John's birthday cake was baked in the wood stove at the Wall Canyon cow camp every year since he was seven during the spring gather, mid-June. Perfect, if you're a boy. Cow camp with the men, their talk, their cooking, their work.

Just at daybreak, the water whap, whap of the sage grouse drumming in the canyon just above the cabin would wake him. Slipping through the brush, the last part crawling, he would get a look at the cocks strutting, hens on the sideline. Later on, the chance of seeing antelope in the basin west of Badger Mountain where they came to kid in the short brush below the spring.

Now it was my turn. John gave me the outside swing up Greasy Flat toward the sound he described, toward the basin where I might see courting and birth.

The antelope kid exploded from under my horse, not as a land mine detonated by weight, its survival instinct triggered before the hoof touched it. Horse, antelope shot in opposite directions. I got my horse stopped and pointed at a wobbling dot as it disappeared off the edge of the earth.

Heart-sick, I worried all day long about the little antelope wandering the breaks, bleating for a tall blur and smell that was Mother and not finding her. I was lost at the Washington State Fair when I was a kid, not wise enough to ask for help, looking for a pink flowered dress and a pair of Levis in a forest of hemlines and Levis. On a Nevada desert rim I was as close to that old desperation as I had ever been.

I knew the doe would have been dehydrated from birthing and cleaning away every trace of membrane. Her body giving again, nursing the kid—precious colostrum, thick with antibodies to neutralize the bacterial flowers in the baby's gut. Nuzzling under the kid's tail, the doe would stimulate the passing of dark, sticky feces, and memorize a scent, a taste, layering it into the patina of her own. The kid, meanwhile, consuming from her udder the same tangible and intangible layers, distinct forever as pepperwood from lily. Then she would have stood, nibbling the short grass on the rocky bench while the kid folded, small enough for a pocket, at her feet. Standing guard she would turn her head, watching, every sense open. When she felt right, a new awareness would waken in her a need for water. She would leave the kid sleeping, safely odorless, nearly invisible to predators and walk to a spring nearby.

It all worked perfectly, naturally, until my horse and I stumbled onto the kid. "It bolted and now it's lost somewhere," I told my husband, John.

"Don't worry. They'll find each other."

"You don't understand. The kid ran off into the breaks. The doe won't know where to look."

"Mothers always know where to look," he said calmly. "They go back to the beginning."

Impatient with his unconcern I shot back, "Okay. Where *is* the beginning?"

"Anytime a mother and baby get separated they always, always, go back to the place they sucked last. It's built in. No question." He let that soak in a minute. "It's why we mother-up cows and calves every time we change pastures. If the calves get confused or scared they won't run clear back to where they were picked up. Wherever they nurse, every time, that's where they find each other."

How could I have lived so closely with animals all my life and not known of this miracle? To return by code to a shared place. A *place* could be significant. Safe. Important beyond the birth. Important through a bond of nourishment.

As we rode through the complex geography of the low desert we gathered the cattle left to graze at will through the spring. The weather had warmed, the days lengthened, the upland feed was ready to be harvested. It was June. We were going onto Badger Mountain. All day long the moving herd built as riders scoured the draws, the long valleys, the swell and swale, pushing toward the center. From a distant ridge a rough of shadows and colors moved before a funnel of dust, and in that mill—like the one of high heeled shoes and boots at the fair where a small girl lost the hand that held hers, the hip she walked beside—the bond of cow and calf was tested. At last there was a fence and a gate thrown back. Armed with a new way of seeing, I learned about "mothering-up." The bawling cows turned back, the calves darted away or stood, battered with confusion. Riders pulled away. We held them loosely and gave them time to order their thinking. The process can take an hour, more. The elements of survival rise slow as cream. The cowman may seem to be doing nothing, sitting on his tired horse, watching. But he is playing the card game Concentration, matching a pair of jacks (brayford cow and the white necked calf), a pair of tens (black cow that calved in the lake field and her black baldy calf), a pair of threes (straight Hereford pair). Good cowmen don't rely on numbered eartags; they *know* their cattle. Good mothers search the herd, smelling every calf until hers is found and nurses. It went on until we were satisfied every match had been made. Only then we counted our work done and let the cattle graze away. But there can be a mix-up. The next morning a rider would go back to that gate. If any cows with tight bags or any calves were hanging along the fence or bawling through the wires the rider would assume they had not mothered-up or that one half of the pair had been missed in the drive the day before. He would open the gate to let them go back to pair up at the last place they sucked.

A few years after the incident with the kid antelope the theory was tested again. The outcome was all the proof I would ever need. Mid-May we shipped a load of dry cows to the desert. They would calve in the low country. In June we would brand all the longeared calves as we moved them up to their summering country. When the truck came up the road at first light we had already gathered the meadow and were pushing them into the crowding alley. We loaded the truck, sent it off, and rode to a field in the foothills to work out pairs for the next load. When we came in for lunch there was a calf bawling in the meadow we had gathered in that early morning dark. One of the drys had calved during the night. We had mistakenly put her on the truck and sent her sixty miles east. Her baby bawled from the willows. There was nothing to do then. The trucker had unloaded hours before and the cow could have been anywhere in the Yellow Hills. But John's faith in our cows was deep and abiding. He looked at his watch and did some figuring. "She'll be back by about 2:00 a.m." At 2:30 a.m. the dogs barked. John got up, pulled his boots on, walked out to the yard, opened the gate and let the cow into the meadow. She went bawling off in the darkness. In those hours she had walked out of the belly of the cattle truck, allowed her mind to locate a direction, and started back through the day and into the night. She did not wail and wander circles from the chute gate. She was a needle compassed, charged by a distant point. While a world spun on around her, she moved through a tunnel of her own making. Steady, steady. Across the desert she sipped water from catch pools, snatched at bunch grass and went on. Over the treacherous barriers of cattle-guards,

she was light-footed. Up the mountain pass, she did not falter. At Lake
Surprise, she walked water. There was no dotted line on pavement, no
road signs for her. She followed the pledge of an internal map to a place
anchored in an event revisited by the female of every nurturing species.

Our breed goes to the baby's crib when it cries, holds the baby as it
suckles because it is not developed fully at birth and cannot come to us.
Later we call the child indoors, the family together, for meals, and
strengthen our comfort in communion-talk, nearness as nourishing as
food. We return to the one place that can satisfy our needs for company,
rest, encouragement. Nature gave us the right response. Like wild things
we are born knowing. As children we collect important information about
our surroundings while we putter and play, seemingly engaged with col-
ored blocks and rings. I imagine the alignment of chemicals within the
brain to identify this spot, this place for all times. And if that alignment
is interrupted the search may go on indefinitely.

Children sew through the out-of-doors like butterflies, touching down,
tasting, learning their place. They come home when they're hungry. Their
pockets bulge with pretty stones, acorns, string, a bird skull, a bent nail.
All of these treasures are their connections to the world. Each has a
story of discovery, how it came to be where little hands could grasp it. If
the parents have forgotten their own graceful entry to the pleasures of
centering the self, all of it may be tossed in the trash.

At a certain age we stop sifting the earth with our fingers, the air with
our bodies, as we are told to stop drawing dreamy pictures and tend to
our homework. We begin weaning from the wholeness of the natural
life, selecting different paths that turn toward a kind of isolation.

At some point most of us look to reestablish our animal sense of secu-
rity that was set aside. Sensing its loss, we drag things to us hoping to
find the *right* thing. We search on through body, mind, illusion. Nour-
ishment of the whole being has dwindled to an ephemeral memory. Noth-
ing can take the place of the last place the bond was secured.

The antelope kid ran in alarm, frightened by a strange nearness that
might have been fatal. Soon it stopped and laid down. After a while,
when it was quieted, messages began again. Surreal (it wound a thread
as fine, as stout as water's memory of its source—light's hot wink of
ignition—a cant of sound from stone to seed, from seed to time and back—
all this and more: vaporous, yet, fixed, recalled ever after), drawing the
kid on kindling legs to the holy ground where nourishment was given—
and Mother, waiting.

TWO MOUNTAIN STONES:
COWBOY CHARACTER STUDIES

PREFACE

I'm frequently asked, "Still writing the poems?"

I answer, "Well, yes. Some. But mostly I've been writing prose instead."

Why have I moved away from a form that has been successful for me, and which I understand? Maybe "boredom" is the answer, or part of it at least. I'm bored with the overpopulation of "bunkhouse bards" that have invaded the cowboy poetry movement without having any understanding of either syntax, meter or cowboy culture. I'm bored with both fans and critics of cowboy poetry who praise or condemn the genre without any consideration of quality of writing. And maybe, just maybe, I'm embarrassed that my most popular poem, "Reincarnation" is, after all, just a joke that my college roommate, Sid Griffith, told me that I twisted into rhyme and meter, while several other poems, that I feel reflect better writing and themes, are ignored.

My good friend/severe critic, Paul Zarzyski *ordered* me to write down some of these stories that I had been telling him for years. "I've been trying to do just that," I responded, "but some of them just don't want to be written as poems."

"Write them down just like you tell them, then. Look, you're old, you've had a quadruple heart bypass, you don't take good care of yourself, and you're going to die without getting them written down. Just write the damn things down in a conversational way," Paul said.

"But, Paul, I don't know the first thing about writing prose," I protested.

"You sure know how to talk. Write 'em like you're talking. Just do it," he said.

So the prose pieces that I've been writing are, in the final analysis, Zarzyski's fault.

I have often compared individual characters in a rural culture to rocks that have recently crashed down a mountainside. Like talus slope boulders, they have not been tumbled into conformity by society. The true rural characters—most don't even realize that they are characters—are all sharp-edged, irregular with unworn surfaces unlike stream-tumbled boulders that might be of different shapes, colors and sizes, but are smoothed and rounded by constantly being rolled into conformity, by grinding against their close neighbors into a monotonous sameness.

About twenty years ago, a neighbor, Jack Bradley, and I built us a new house. We used several truckloads of native rocks. The rocks had been tempered by prehistoric fires into sharp flint, scotia and chert and bubbled into porous, jagged clinkers. Compared to river-smoothed boulders, some would consider them ugly, difficult to shape and handle, and impossible to erect into respectable fireplaces and walls. Like some of the characters that I write about, they are rough, but they are genuine.

COWMAN

You couldn't describe him as a perfectionist in all areas. We built a dog house for a mutt of contorted pedigree named "Zip" one time. Maybe we could blame our tools: a dull crosscut saw, a shoeing hammer, some rough-cut, warped, one-inch boards, and some re-straightened nails of various sizes. We did okay with the floor and the sides, but once that part of the construction was completed, we tackled the roof. We finally settled on a sort of modified, flat-pitched roof that we planned to nail to the irregular height sides. Since nothing was square, there were big gaps just below the eaves. We thought we could stuff some chunks of rags in the holes in order to keep the weather out. We had plenty of rags. The wife and mother of the construction crew had grudgingly donated an old "car blanket" to serve as a winter bed for the dog. We were pretty proud when the project was finished. The problem was old Zip wouldn't enter his new diggings. Oh, if we baited him with choice tidbits from the table, he would cautiously sneak into the crude opening, snatch the offered snack, roll over his hocks and dart out to eat the morsel between the clematis vines and the concrete house foundation. My dad and I concluded that some dogs, Zip included, were "outside dogs" and possessed such amazing grit that they didn't need a shelter even in the harshest weather.

My son, Clint, really understands an internal combustion engine and all of the components that constitute vehicles. Unless it is a modern "black box" computer problem, he can diagnose and repair all sorts of machines. I can assure you that Clint didn't get his automotive talent from his paternal grandfather, however. My dad viewed all machines with superstition and fear. He would try to appease the mechanical gods by faithfully anointing various species of the genus "Machinus" with great gobs of Conoco grease and by religiously topping off the radiator, battery and oil sump. But if a machine began to sputter, he would run it until it quit, check the various fluid levels and walk home.

But my father did understand livestock. Especially cattle. We would be moseying along, trailing cows and calves to the leases on the Cheyenne Reservation, in the spring, and he would ride back to my position in the drags and say, "Come up here." I would follow him up the side of the herd and he would gesture towards a stream of red and white cattle and say, "Remember that red eyed cow?"

"Which one?" I'd ask, knowing that I was about to fail his test.

"That one with the red spot on her front leg. Remember her?"

"Which one?"

"That one right there following the yellow cow with the good bull calf."

"I think I remember her," I'd bluff, not even sure which cow he was pointing out. And he would go into a soliloquy concerning some obscure event that happened when the cow was a calf. He would then reminisce about her whole family, including her mother, his speculation on which bull—long since shipped—sired her, her past calves and siblings.

"That cow with the white tuft on top her neck is her sister. Two, no, three years younger," he'd report cautiously, so as not to offend me if I already knew this impossibly obscure information. "I'll ride back to the drags with you," he'd say. "We'll tuck them in on the way back—against the grain. That works best."

He would constantly coach me on position, or the distance that I should keep my horse from the cattle. Usually, I was too close. "Back off a bit," he'd say.

It was always a mistake, but sometimes I would argue, or plead my case, with him. "But you're closer than I am."

"That's because I'm better mounted than you are," he'd explain. "This horse can get back faster than yours." Acknowledging that my "Buck," "Snooper" or "Whitey" was a slow, hard-mouthed, lazy plug of a kid horse. Or, if we were corralling a herd and they were starting to mill, "Move up. Move up. But not too close. Don't let any calves squirt out," he'd caution.

He would often quote cowboy scripture from the local prophet, Josh McCuistion: "It's a damn poor outfit where everybody rides behind." Or "Cattle are a string. If you try to push a string, it'll get all wadded up. But you can pull a string anywhere." "Let the leaders pull the drags, don't try to mash the drags through 'em." "One man can drive one cow. Two men can drive two cows. Three men can trail two hundred." Or if a couple of riders — usually kids — holding herd were bored with the job and sat visiting: "If you two are going to ride the same horse, you might as well turn one loose and let him graze." "Start a herd by letting the leaders trail out. They're the smoke that draws the fire along. Push on the coals and you're gonna get burned."

Of course some quotes from "The Book of Josh" were not instructive, just entertaining. If a horse would stumble, then get gathered up and run off a bit: "Like Josh says, 'I can forgive a horse for stumbling, but I wish he'd stop apologizing for it.'" Or if a horse would suddenly shy at a shoulder-high, ten-ton rock alongside a trail: "Like Josh says, 'You hands go ahead and laugh, but somebody threw a rock at this horse one time that looked a whole lot like that one.'" Perhaps the best one was both humorous and a caution. If a roper was having a hard time heeling calves, or if someone let his horse get out of position either working the herd, or corralling cattle and caused an embarrassing wreck, someone would recall the quote from Josh: "Fight your horse, that'll help. Seen lotsa fellas do it."

Occasionally my dad would holler at me, in front of other people, for some cattle-handling sin. "Now you stay awake, and turn back for me when I'm cutting something out," he would instruct me loudly from deep in the herd. This was done in the typically oblique way of instructing someone other than the accused. Later, when we were alone, he would bring it up. "You know why I got on you for not figuring out the deal on turning back for me today?" he'd ask.

"I wasn't doing my job?" I'd guess.

"No. You were doing fine," he'd say, "but Carp was so busy admiring his shadow that he wasn't making a hand, so I hollered at you to wake him up. After that he made a hand, for a while. Did you notice?"

"No," I'd say.

"Well he did. You should pay attention, Boy."

It's unfortunate, I believe, that "Boy" has become a diminishing or pejorative term. When my father used it, "Boy" was a compliment. It meant that I was not only a son of which he was proud, but that I was an apprentice for whom he held high, but attainable, expectations. "Boy" was a good word.

Shortly after I learned to read, my dad gave me a small book with gilt edged pages. It was titled "Don'ts For Boys." The book's green, soft leather cover was torn, and many of the pages had come loose from the spine. My grandmother had given it to him. It's well-worn appearance was a result of much use, not abuse or misuse. It was filled with Victorian instructions on etiquette, decorum and manners. He encouraged me to read it, and occasionally would either read some of it to me or question me on its contents. He especially liked me to ask questions about some of the rules in the book. It was important, not only that I be a "good boy," but that I understand the purpose behind the rule.

My mother and father could have co-authored another book at about that same time. "Don'ts For Young Cowboys" would have been an appropriate title. "Don't tie a horse up to something he can drag," one of them would suggest. A hair-raising, perhaps true, story would follow about some fool who tied his halter rope to a buggy seat and of the crippled horse that resulted from a runaway. "Don't tie your horse up with the bridle reins," was another. "Don't ride between someone else and the herd." "Don't touch the canvas on a wet roundup tent." "Keep your latigo pulled tight through the keeper." "Don't be the first one in line at the chuck wagon." "Don't play with matches in the hayloft." "Don't use a stout rope strap on your saddle." The list was endless, appropriate and interesting. Even more impressive were some of the "don'ts" that my parents had failed to observe and the consequences: Such as the time my dad put the loop of a lariat around his waist and tied the far end to a post. He soon forgot about being picketed, goosed and boogered like the wild horse that he was pretending to be, had a runaway that resulted in him passing blood for several days. Or the time my mother's sister, Marion, saw a rattlesnake and picked up a big rock with which to dispatch it but failed to notice another snake curled around the rock. Marion rode several miles home with a bridle rein wrapped so tightly around her bitten finger that there was some consideration given to amputation. I knew that there was a lesson there, but I'm still not sure if it had to do with checking rocks for lurking snakes, or not applying a rein tourniquet too tightly or for too long.

I suppose I learned more about being a good hand before I ever began receiving a formal, school education. Schooling interfered with learning to be a cowboy. During branding, gathering, calving and shipping I was often too busy getting "an education." Only occasionally would my cowboy lessons be resumed.

Once when I was in college, my father came to Bozeman, where I was attending school, and picked me up to go look at some bulls at Monforton's Ranch out in the Gallatin Valley. "What do you think, Boy?" he asked as we slogged through pens of bulls.

"Number one oh four. What about that one?" I'd ask, relieved for the moment from writing down numbers branded into the horns of coming two-year old Hereford bulls that he had selected for possible purchase.

His mouth would purse into a straight horizontal line as he studied the bull that I had indicated. "Too chuffy," he'd say, using a term that I had never heard before.

"Chuffy?" I'd ask.

"Yah, chuffy. No stretch or scale. Put him out on short grass with a bunch of cows and he'd render down to a little pot-bellied wharf rat. He's fat. Fat's a good color, but that's all. Remember that."

"Chuffy?" "Fat's a good color?" The lessons required some translation, but were good advice.

After college, I went into the Navy. While I was in the service, my father died. There were so many things that I wished I had learned when I struck out on my own. But some of the things that I learned from my father only required some adaptation in order to be valuable.

One summer, when I was probably ten years old, my dad and I were out riding, checking on the cattle, their water and fences. We were on Lee Coulee, where Peabody Coal Company is mining now, and ran across a bunch of Jim Bailey's yearling heifers mixed in with our cows and calves. We found a hole in the fence on top of a small rise where all of the staples had come out of the cedar post and had let the wires down to the ground. Dad had some staples in his saddle pocket, but we scoured the ground until we found the four that had come out of the post—no use using new ones when, with a little time, we could scrounge the used ones. I held the wires in place while Dad pounded the staples in with a rock. I'm pretty sure he checked for snakes before picking up his geological "hammer."

"Let's see if we can get those heifers back in Bailey's," Dad suggested. "We'll throw them down next to the fence. You can hold the herd and turn back for me. I'll cut the yearlings out real easy, and you can hold them sorta loose. Otherwise they'll be all over the pasture and we'll have to ride it all, later, to get them back in. We can do it. Don't ya think?"

Every fiber in my mind and body screamed, "No!" to his question. "Maybe," I said.

Twenty minutes later, my throat was raw with frustration and suppressed tears, and he was beginning to holler. "Easy. Easy! The cut is getting away! Come back here and turn that cow back! Spur that horse in the belly and get him to move!"

Although I'm sure it is mentioned in "Don'ts For Boys," I finally screamed back. "I'm doing the best I can. I've got three jobs: Hold the herd. Turn back. And hold the cut. I can't do it all!"

Then my dad said something that, if it could be phrased in a negative or cautionary way, would fit in the "Don'ts For Young Cowboys" book and be pretty good general advice in life. He said, "Keep moving, Boy. Cows can't count."

ALBERT TALLBULL

Albert's son, Jacob, was a classmate of mine during my senior year in high school. Jacob, and a couple of his Indian friends, Lafe Harris, and Steven Two Two, decided that they would star for three different basketball teams, and having played for two of the other schools in our district, climbed on the yellow bus headed for Colstrip for their senior year. That way they would have three different letter sweaters, emblazoned with three different school logos, in their wardrobes. Because the newcomers were transfer students, they were prohibited from playing for our team until the second semester. After the Christmas break, I was relegated to ride the bench for the rest of the year. That was okay with me. I was a sorry basketball player, and the introduction of fresh talent considerably raised the quality of our team. Besides I genuinely liked the new additions and, what the hell, I was a football player.

As soon as Jacob was able to begin playing, his father, Albert, and his stepmother, Rilla, started attending our games. I therefore developed a nodding acquaintance with the senior Tallbulls. Naturally there was a bit of a strain in our relationship. After all, this was the fifties, they were old, their son had replaced me as a starter, and they were Indians.

I received an early release from the Navy after my father died. I had been away from home for seven years, in college and in the service, and was somewhat surprised at the ebullience with which Albert greeted me when I ran into him at James King's Standard service station, until I realized that he was reflecting the respect that the Cheyennes show for returning military personnel. "Ho! Sojer boy," Albert said, offering a respectfully limp hand for me to shake.

"How's Jacob?" I asked.

"Oh, you know. Drunk," said Albert.

"Where is he?"

"Over there at the jail," Albert said, pointing with his lips.

"That's too bad," I said.

"No. Jacob's no good."

"He was a good basketball player."

Albert shook his head. "Yes. Two things Jacob's good at: Play basketball. And drink."

After that we developed a sort of strange but comfortable relationship. I was interested in collecting Cheyenne crafts and artifacts, and in understanding the nuances of their culture and religion. My side of the symbiotic equation came in supplying some of the necessities of life and requirements that Albert had in his religious quests. Albert would drive down and give me an old ceremonial icon. "I thought you needed this," Albert would say, handing me a buffalo hide rattle incised with strange symbols.

"What's this?" I'd ask.

"It's a rattle."

"What's it for?"

"It's an old rattle that those old guys used to use. There's lots of spirits in it. But we forgot how to use it, and those spirits might be mad if we did things wrong, so I thought you should have it."

"Is it going to bring me bad luck?" I'd ask.

"I don't know. Maybe. Do you want it?"

"Sure. I'll take the chance, but if I break my leg again I'll blame you," I'd joke.

Completely seriously, Albert would say, "I think you'll be okay."

Then it was my turn. "Need anything?" I'd ask.

"I need some spare beef. Maybe liver. Twenty-seven dollars, fill that gas tank, some 650 X 15 tires, two, maybe three, five gallon cans of gas and seven quarts real heavy oil," he'd dictate his shopping list.

"Big trip," I'd say. "Where you going this time?"

"It's time to go down to that Texas and get the peyote," he'd reply, peyote being the mildly hallucinogenic cactus that is a sacrament in the Native American Church.

"Will your list get you there and back?"

"I will stay with those guys down in that Oklahoma and they will help out," he'd confidently, and, to me, mysteriously, reply.

Although we didn't keep track, I'm sure that, value for value, things evened out. Sometimes he would borrow back some of the articles that were traded, and I would ask if he needed to keep the item. "No. It's yours. I'll bring it back," he'd usually say. But, occasionally he'd reply, "I better keep this one. I'll get you a better one." And maybe he would.

I finally realized that my specifically requesting a certain item was a violation of our tacit agreement, but prior to that understanding, I asked for a pipe. I had in mind a Minnesota pipestone platform, or "T" shaped one with a squared wooden stem, an admittedly "touristy" item. Long after I had given up on my order, Albert brought me a pipe. I was disappointed that instead of being a platform pipe it was an undecorated "straight" pipe. Years later someone, who knew much more than I about Indian artifacts, asked where I had gotten the pipe, after noting, with surprise, that it had been "smoked." I was amazed to learn that the plain straight pipe was used only in the sun dance and, because this one had been smoked, that it had been used during the most sacred of Cheyenne ceremonies.

On another occasion, when the shopping list was quite short, maybe just some "spare beef" and "a few dollars." I asked, "What's up?"

"It's for a peyote meeting," Albert said.

"Where is it going to be held?"

"At my place."

"Could I come?" I asked, realizing the boldness of my request as soon as it was spoken.

After a long pause, with a whole lot of horizon gazing—to let me know that the question was a violation of both of our codes of conduct—Albert asked, "Would I be welcome in your church?"

With what we both knew was probably a lie, I said, "Sure."

After another long pause, Albert said, "It's about dark on Tuesday. You can come."

I'm ashamed that my curiosity eclipsed my sense of propriety, and I went. I'm still humbled by the degree of respect with which I was received, and wonder if Albert's reception would have been as gracious as mine was, in my church, or if I would have been as forgiving of gross, if unintended, violations of religious piety.

On another occasion, having been presented with a middle-sized request list, I asked, "Where to this time, Albert?"

"It's a prayer meeting down to Bear Butte," he stated, naming the most holy site in the Cheyenne religion.

"What happens there?" I asked.

"Oh I don't know. We just go down there to that South Dakota, go up on Bear Butte and pray."

"Any special reason for this prayer trip?"

"Oh yah. This is for the sojer boys over at that Viet Nam. Lots of Cheyenne boys over there. And then we pray for The People; for the old ones and the sick ones and the little ones and for our good white rancher neighbors that help us when we need it. And like that."

I badgered Albert with all sorts of questions about the preparations, the cleansing ceremonies, the fasting and whether they used group or individual prayer while communicating with the spirits.

"We're all sorta together up there maybe, but we talk to those spirits without speaking. Like we were alone, I guess."

I knew that I was being rude, but I asked, "Do you think your prayers are ever answered?"

"Oh sure."

"How do you know?"

"One time those spirits talked to me!"

"How did that come about?" I asked.

"Well it was that third day. I was really hot and thirsty but there were big clouds coming up. There was thunder and lightning in those clouds, so I knew that those spirits were up there too. And those clouds came right over us, and the thunder was real close. That grass all laid down and pointed at me like it was little ears, so I knew that those spirits were listening and I prayed really hard. And a little hole opened up, and just a little bit of sun came down on top of Bear Butte, no place else. And those spirits then they talked to me!"

"Was it in Cheyenne language? What did the voices say?" I asked.

"I don't know. I was sitting beside that Waldo. He smokes them Winston cigarettes and got one of those coughing fits and I never did hear what they say."

To this day I haven't decided if Albert was telling the truth, or if the story was his subtle way of informing me that my prying questions were offensive and not deserving of a serious answer.

I don't know if it was caused by some of the bad spirits originating from some of his "medicine objects" that I received from Albert, but I managed to regularly break my left leg. Just after I had the second of three horse wrecks resulting in a broken leg—in six years—a neighbor of mine, Jack Bailey, ran into Albert at the "Big Store" in Lame Deer and said, "Albert. What's the news?"

"Oh, I don't know. Wally McRae broke that leg," Albert suggested.

"That's not news. He broke it a couple of years ago," Jack stated.

"Well I just heard he broke it."

"How did it happen?"

"Well this horse slipped down and skidded on it and broke it right off,

I heard."

"No. That was a couple of years ago."

"Oh yah. I guess he's in that hospital up at Billin's. Somebody saw him up there yesterday."

"In Billings?" Jack said. "You sure? He had the last one fixed in Miles City."

"Yup. He's up there in that Billin's."

"I'll be damned. Same horse?" Jack asked.

"No. This was that other sorrel horse."

"Break both bones again?"

"Yup, both bones in the same leg again, this guy said."

"Break it in the same place?" Jack asked, thinking the worst.

"No," Albert said. "It was about six miles east of there." They both had a good laugh.

Funny guy, Albert. I was busy doing something that I thought was more important on the day of his funeral, but he probably didn't need my attendance. I used to take some "spare meat" up to Rilla every once in a while until she joined Albert. We'd just sit, drink coffee and mostly think about Albert until it was time for me to go.

ESSAYS

BORDERLANDS:
COWBOY POETRY AND THE LITERARY CANON

One of the most frustrating aspects of discussing cowboy poetry is what might be called the "you had to be there" response. Really. You had to be there — Elko, Nevada, the last weekend in January at the Cowboy Poetry Gathering. To pick up a book of classic cowboy poems and read Bruce Kiskaddon's "When They Finish Shipping Cattle in the Fall" is an incomplete experience. You need to see ex-cowboss Waddie Mitchell recite it. You need to hear rancher poet Linda Hussa recite, "Under Hunter Moon," her soft voice a counterpoint to the first line of her poem: "I slip the rifle sling over my shoulder and step into the silence of dawn." You cannot get the full measure of "The Heavyweight Champion Pie Eatin' Cowboy of the West" when you read it. You need to hear the lusty comic intonations of cowboy poet and rodeo rider Paul Zarzyski as he recites it. And be prepared to shed a tear when Texan Joel Nelson recites "Anthem," the great poem of the much-mourned cowboy poet Buck Ramsey. It is this orality that relegates cowboy poetry to the borderlands. However interesting on the page, these poems cry out for recitation. A literary canon is a body of written texts, not performances.

Where in the literary canon does cowboy poetry belong? Does anyone in the literary world care? While the popular press has been fascinated by the success of cowboy poetry and the seeming paradox of the cowboy poet, literary critics, for the most part, have been silent. It is, however, time to consider the fundamental question of cowboy poetry's literary identity. I propose to begin this task by examining three important notions: the essential orality of cowboy poetry, some recent themes in the genre, and the persona of the cowboy poet.

My inquiry is based primarily on my observations over the years attending the Cowboy Poetry Gathering in Elko, Nevada; the programs, which have always contained both scholarly articles by state and university folklorists and good biographical notes of the cowboy poet presenters; more than thirty audio tapes I have collected of cowboy poetry sessions; and the work of poet and critic Dana Gioia, author of *Can Poetry Matter? Essays on Poetry and American Culture* and co-editor with X.J. Kennedy of *Introduction to Poetry*, a standard college textbook that actually mentions cowboy poetry, Gioia also kindly allowed me to use an unpublished paper, "Poetry at the End of Print Culture," which he first

presented as a Fales Lecture at New York University, invaluable in find-
ing a fresh approach to the phenomenon of cowboy poetry.

Gioia puts the problem of orality into a larger context when he says,
"Just as European literature changed two and a half millennia ago as it
moved from oral to written culture, so has popular poetry transformed
itself as it moves from print culture to our audio-visual culture in which
writing exists but is no longer the primary means of public discourse."[1]
He goes on to say that this epistemological change "transforms the iden-
tity of the author from writer to entertainer, from an invisible creator of
typographic language to a physical presence performing aloud."[2] He also
notes that "these new popular forms emerged outside literary life."[3] "Out-
side" is the key word here. If these forms were not learned primarily
through print sources and as part of a standard poetry canon, where
were they learned? Or, as a cowboy poet would say, "How do you come
by a good poem?"

One of the most famous quotes referring to the oral dissemination of
cowboy poetry is by Will James from his book *Cow Country* published in
1927: "Then in the evenings there'd be songs, old trailherd songs that
some used to sing. There was even poetry at times, made right there at
the cowcamp. It'd always be about some cowboy and some bad horse,
and the whole outfit chipped in or suggested a word to make it up."[4] In
the documentary video *Cowboy Poets* popular cowboy poet Waddie
Mitchell tells a more recent anecdote of the same kind. "It was awful
hard to come by a good poem," he says, and then tells the story of
cowboying on an outfit where one of the hands, "an old guy named
Keckie," recited a poem in the bunkhouse that had these "rough tough
men that I idolized" moved to tears, or at least staring at the floor. Mitchell
says, "I just knew I had to have that poem."[5]

I gleaned from program notes, primarily in 1986, other examples of
how presenters featured at the Gathering learned cowboy poetry.[6] Over
fifty cowboy poets from eighteen states presented that year. Cowboy
poet Ernie Fanning, from Fernley, Nevada, "picked up much of his large
repertoire of cowboy poems from other cowboys." Fanning says "you
had to teach one to learn one" and this sometimes led to all-night swap-
ping sessions. Bill "Blackie" Black, from Adel, Oregon, " . . . learned his
first three bunkhouse poems at the Ellison Ranch in Nevada." Bob
Johnston, from Scottsbluff, Nebraska, says, "He heard cowboys recite
poetry while he was growing up in the bunkhouses and after a day's

work on the ranch. He recalls rodeo cowboys singing and reciting in bars, in their pickups, and on casual occasions." Ross Knox, from Seligman, Arizona, developed a keen interest in cowboy poems which he heard old-timers recite in bars around Nevada. Leon Flick, from Plush, Oregon, first heard cowboy poems . . . at brandings and "as a kid, at the Plush general store." Presenters frequently mentioned family traditions. Yula Sue Whipple Hunting, from Beryl, Utah, says that "for at least four generations my family has written and recited poems." Some acknowledged their mothers as bearers of this oral culture. Charles A. Kortes, of Rawlins, Wyoming, states his poetry was "influenced by his mother." Don Bowman, of Fallon, Nevada, mentions his "grandmother who recited cowboy poetry."

Not all cowboy poetry was passed on orally. The print sources, however, were never part of the literary canon. For example, well-known Montana cowboy poet Wallace McRae says that "we liked poetry in our home back in the '40s when my sister, Marjorie, used to cut poems out of a livestock publication and glue them to a pale blue hair ribbon and hang them by a straight pin in her room."[7] Nevada cowboy Stan Lehman speaks of "his father's copy of Curley Fletcher's 'Songs of the Sage'" and recalls seeing poetry in a magazine called Ranch Romance when he was young. Many cowboys referred to the older "cowboy canon that is, the recitations of Bruce Kiskaddon, Badger Clark, Gail Gardner, S. Omar Barker, and Curley Fletcher. Typical of this oral apprenticeship is Richard Smith, of Carson City, Nevada, whose interest in cowboy poetry began with a book of Bruce Kiskaddon's work. Later he became acquainted with the poetry of Curley Fletcher, Gail Gardner, and Robert Service. American humorist Will Rogers exemplifies this tradition. "Will's study was next to our room upstairs in the east end of the house. Books of cowboy songs and old ranch poetry were there. He bought every one he heard about. It was easy for him to memorize and he like to recite 'Sam Bass,' 'Hell in Texas,' and 'On the Banks of the Cimarron,'"says his wife in her 1941 biography.[8]

Some cowboy poets come from the more mainstream tradition of writing occasional verse. Barney Nelson, from Alpine, Texas, says, "I don't really consider myself a poet. I just write poems for our Christmas cards or to give with gifts to friends." Paul Schmitt, in Stagecoach, Nevada, also says he started writing songs and poems for friends. Others state that they wrote cowboy poetry simply for their own amusement. Jesse Smith, of Porterville, California, says "for lack of TV or radio," he started writing verse. Georgie Sicking, of Fallon, Nevada, states, "I guess it was loneliness that started me making up poems—living by myself, without

much to read, I had a lot of time to think." Vess Quinlan, who lives in
Alamosa, Colorado, says, "I kept my interest in poetry pretty much to
myself in the early years. Afraid, I guess, someone or everyone would
make fun of the idea of making poems." Bill Sullivan, of Sheridan, Mon-
tana, recalls that he would "memorize the poems and then recite them to
myself as I rode the trail."

This last image of Bill Sullivan in the Montana back country "riding
and reciting" may be true to the reality of this oral tradition, but it doesn't
fit with the cowboy myth. Jim Griffith, Director of the Southwest Folk-
lore Center at the University of Arizona, asks the question, "Why has
recitation never been given the place in the cowboy myth that singing
has? The singing cowboy has become a commonplace Western image;
the poetry-reciting cowboy is still a strange figure to outsiders."[9] He
then gives some possible answers:

> In the first place, singing is a much more romantic occupation than
> recitation, which smacks, to outsiders, of the schoolroom and par-
> lor. But even cowboys once went to school and the skills one learns
> in one's youth may be put to use in a number of ways later on. Sing-
> ing to the cattle on night guard caught the imagination of readers of
> western stories; ballad singing was what folklorists of 70 years ago
> were looking for.

> For these and other reasons, cowboy songs became an important
> part of the Western image, while cowboy recitations were (and still
> are) largely unheard of . . . . "[10]

In the same article, Griffith gives further insights into the cultural tradi-
tions of recitation and their relationship to cowboy poetry:

> A hundred years ago, reciting poetry was a lot more widespread
> than it is today. In the first place, memorizing verses and reciting
> them was something school kids had to do. In the second, there wasn't
> the specialization we have in our society today. Poetry and many of
> the other art forms turned a corner in the early 1900s and became
> less and less accessible to the general public.[11]

Finally, the Cowboy Poetry Gathering itself has been an inspiration and impetus to cowboy poets and reciters. After attending the 1987 Elko Gathering, cowboy poet Kent Stockton, of Riverton, Wyoming, went home and organized the Wyoming Poetry Gathering. Bill Lowman, of Sentinel Butte, North Dakota, who says "I was writing cowboy rhymes for my own amusement long before the Elko Gathering," became the founder and director of the popular Dakota Poetry Gathering. Any number of ranch men and women had an experience similar to that of Connie Satterthwaite, from Tuscarora, Nevada, who came to the first Gathering in 1985, went back to the ranch inspired to write her own cowboy poetry, and has been a frequent presenter ever since.

So, these were the major ways today's cowboy poets came by their literary models: first, they heard them on the ranch, relaxing after work in the ranch house, bunkhouse, or at a bar; second, because recitation was a tradition in their families and they "just always heard" classics of the cowboy canon; third, they read the cowboy poetry in livestock magazines, or other rural publications; or, finally, since 1985, they attended the Cowboy Poetry Gathering in Elko, Nevada.

How does this essential orality affect the stature of cowboy poetry within the literary establishment? Several responses come to mind. One is to view cowboy poetry as a cultural artifact, a folk tradition like country fiddling or horsehair rope braiding. In some ways, the very creation of the Cowboy Poetry Gathering lends support to this view. The first reading of cowboy poetry in Elko was organized by a local community college art instructor, as part of an interest in ranch crafts and traditions. However, it was state and university folklorists, not art departments or English departments, who established the first Cowboy Poetry Gathering in 1985—and then were amazed by the vitality of what they found. Hal Cannon, long-time director of the Western Folklife Center, expert on folklife of the Great Basin, and one of the founders of the Gathering, said in the 1986 program, "When I first started working on cowboy poetry—reading it, collecting it, meeting the people who write it—I had no idea there was so much of it . . . ."[12] In many ways this "discovery" of cowboy poetry seems part of the cultural movements of the late 1960's to preserve traditional folkways. Cannon reinforces this when he says the following:

> The folklorists who organized the Gathering—who wrote letters to the editors of country papers, who looked through libraries for old books of cowboy poetry, who drove the backroads to get acquainted with the best cowboy poets they could find—care about cowboy po-

etry because of its strong sense of tradition. It's a form of expression
that reflects the broad experience of most ranch people, and it also
has strong links to the past."[13]

A second, slightly more literary approach is to see cowboy poetry as
folk poetry. This perspective is emphasized by the 1997 focus of the
Gathering. Billed as the "Celtic Connection," the Gathering featured the
poetry and storytelling traditions of the drover cultures of Ireland and
Wales; 1998 focused on oral folk traditions in Scotland and England.
The verbal virtuosity of the Irish and the Welsh habit of poetry-making
for all kinds of occasions made a case for the kinship between cowboy
poetry and traditional Celtic storytelling and poetry. Other commonali-
ties include the prestige conferred upon the cowboy or the crofter with
an extensive oral repertoire and the fact that, in both cultures, the tradi-
tions are more likely perpetuated in the pub and parlor than in the class-
room.

A third approach is text-based but strongly evaluative: cowboy poetry
as light popular verse with little craft and less substance, in other words,
doggerel. In this argument, popularity becomes evidence of superficial-
ity. In "Poetry at the End of Print Culture" Gioia says that, to a certain
faction of literary critics, "the very expression 'popular poetry' sounds
oxymoronic. Trained to identify the art of poetry with high literary cul-
ture, they immediately assume that popular poetry—new or old—is sen-
timental, subliterary drivel—superficial, derivative, or, at best, suavely
mendacious."[14]

Gioia also notes that "the new popular poetry differentiates itself from
mainstream poetry in the most radical way imaginable, by attracting a
huge, paying public."[15] Charlie Seemann, the current director of the
Western Folklife Center in Elko, recently told me that cowboy poet
Baxter Black is the third best-selling poet in America, right behind Dr.
Seuss and Rod McKuen. Good news for Black, who recently bought a
ranch in Arizona; bad news for securing his place in the literary pan-
theon.

The fourth and most thought-provoking response comes from Gioia,
who maintains the new popular poetry, including cowboy poetry, calls
"into question many contemporary assumptions about the current state
of poetry . . . and reflects the broad cultural forces that are now reshap-
ing the literary arts."[16] He thinks that the orality and the popularity of
cowboy poetry are two of the characteristics that place it in the avant

garde. He says that the "four trends that appear so obvious in rap, cow-
boy poetry, and poetry slams—its reliance on oral performance, its non-
academic origins, its revival of auditory form, and its popular appeal—
also exist less overtly in the established literary world."[17] However, he
maintains it is oral transmission versus the medium of print that creates
the strongest distinction between popular poetry and "literary poetry."[18]
About the orality of cowboy poetry, Gioia says that "it hearkens back to
poetry's origins as an oral art form in pre-literate cultures, and it sug-
gests how television, telephones, recordings, and radio have brought most
Americans—consciously or unconsciously—into a new form of oral cul-
ture."[19] Certainly relevant to cowboy poetry is his observation that "the
new popular poetry uses the apparatus of the musical entertainment
world—recordings, radio, concert halls, night clubs, auditoriums, bars,
and festivals."[20]

Gioia also notes the profound relationship between orality and for-
malism:

> . . . the practice of arranging some auditorily apprehensible fea-
> ture such as stress, tone, quantity, alliteration, syllable count, or syn-
> tax into a regular pattern is so universal that it suggests that there is
> something primal and ineradicable at work. Metrical speech not only
> produces some heightened form of attention that increases mne-
> monic retention; it also seems to provide innate physical pleasure in
> both the auditor and orator. Typographic poetry may provide other
> pleasures, but it cannot rewire the circuitry of the human auditory
> perception to change a million years of pre-literate, sensory evolu-
> tion.[21]

Although orality and formalism can be summoned to argue, as Gioia
does, that cowboy poetry's place is in the future, a fifth perspective is to
locate cowboy poetry within "the last Golden Age of poetry,";[22] that is,
within the bardic, Homeric tradition. I would make a case to situate
cowboy poetry in this lineage because of its orality formal structure, and
because of the function of cowboy poetry.

In making a couple of points about the function of cowboy poetry, I
would first claim that, even today, ranch cultures are essentially appren-
ticeship cultures. Professor Walter J. Ong describes such cultures in
Orality and Literacy:

Human beings in primary oral cultures, those untouched by writing in any form, learn a great deal and possess and practice great wisdom, but they do not study." They learn by apprenticeship — hunting with experienced hunters, for example, by discipleship, which is a kind of apprenticeship, by listening, by repeating what they hear, by mastering proverbs and ways of combining and recombining them, by assimilating other formulary materials, by participation in a kind of corporate retrospection — not by study in the strict sense.

Although I would not simplify contemporary ranching business nor suggest that these Westerners are in any way "untouched by writing," I would maintain that in day-to-day ranch work hearing and remembering are critical skills. Learning is more by memory than by memo. I think folklorist Mike Korn alludes to this link between the work and the poetry when he discusses the concept of repetition, mnemonics, and the conservative function of cowboy poetry:

To many who aren't connected with cattle or ranching this repetition (of scenes or motifs) seems redundant. But what these people don't understand is that illustrations such as these "genre" pictures — like cowboy poetry — restate some very basic things about life around cattle and the West. These values, ideas, hazards, problems, jokes, lessons and morals are expressed time after time to teach, fortify, and underline the basic underpinning of a way of life. [23]

The most characteristic feature of oral poetry in the Homeric tradition is its constant repetitions. "They occur at the level of phrase and line (formulas) and whole scenes (typical scenes and themes) and are the building blocks of the oral poet's trade." Furthermore, this oral poetry served the collective memory and welfare of its culture. Although I do not want to overstate my claim, I think there is a valid comparison.[24]

Ranching always has been and still is a communal activity, stereotype of the lone cowboy notwithstanding. I think the bardic and communal nature of cowboy poetry is manifested in two ways: one, being a good reciter and having a lengthy repertoire of memorized poems has tremendous prestige; two, the perpetuation of the repertoire supersedes the importance of the individual poet. Having one's poem become a favorite recitation is more important than pride of authorship. For example,

Wallace McRae's poem, "Reincarnation," immediately became part of the cowboy poetry canon. Although reciters usually acknowledge McRae as the author, it's not a sin if they don't. Colen H. Sweeten, Jr.'s poem, "Dad's Old Hat," is a favorite of cowboy poets. The poem is frequently recited, even on occasions when the poet's name is forgotten. The classic example of the course from authorship, to relative anonymity, to a central place in western folk tradtion is the history of Curley Fletcher's poem, "The Outlaw Bronco," into the "folk" song, "The Strawberry Roan."

I think the aesthetic is effective, Tolstoyan: the function of cowboy poetry is to serve the greater good of the community.[25] Many cowboy poets would essentially agree with the remarks of poet and literary magazine publisher Scott Preston:

> ... poetry in ranchlife has helped braid a much richer expression of culture where visual arts, handicrafts, political discussion, good cooking, physical dexterity and, above all else, serious fellowship are plaited together in a full celebration of being alive. It's an accomplishment that any other school of American poetry should envy. It is where the sacred potential of poems and songs and stories reside. [26]

If oral dissemination is the medium, what about the message? Especially in the last ten years the themes of poetry serve to reinforce the value, and, to a certain extent, bolster the tenuous existence of the culture itself. Cowboy poetry has become increasingly political in its themes. As Nevada cowboy poet Rod McQueary succinctly expresses, "My poetry tries to tell the truth about my culture and my profession. The only thing ranch families can be sure of is that they are misunderstood" And, after reciting "The Lease Hounds" and "Intrinsic Worth," Wallace McRae concludes the *Cowboy Poets* documentary video by looking straight into the camera and saying, "We think that our way of life is important . . . . Who's going to tell our story? Who's going to get across the way we feel to other people?"

In l986, Western Folklife Director Hal Cannon noted the following:

> In recent years cowboy poets have seemed to feel an urgency to let those who work outside the sheep and cattle industries know what it is like to have a way of life threatened by mining, by urbanization, by government policies, by consumer concerns, by environmental concerns — in short by all the pressures of a changing physical and political landscape. [27]

That was more than a decade ago. The issues have intensified. For example, as recent as September 6, 1998, the cover of the *New York Times Book Review* proclaims, "How the West Was Lost" and briefly describes two featured reviews as follows: "'Alienation and Urbanization,' Robert Kaplan says in *An Empire Wilderness* and "'Reckless Exploitation,' according to Timothy Egan in *Lasso the Wind*." In the actual review of *Lasso the Wind*, the reviewer describes Egan as raging against "big ranches, mine owners, dam builders, real estate moguls, timbermen, and, of course, the dead-hand grip still exerted by the Legend of the Old West, which he sees as a 'pitiful excuse for history, a brief shameful period (1846–90) driven by greed, lawlessness and attempted genocide.'"

In a way, the beleaguered status of the family ranch or farm exacerbates the problem of where to place the poetry, ideologically, in the canon. Are we talking about right wing propaganda or the poetry of resistance? Does the conservative function of the poetry necessarily mean a collective, reactionary response, as is the case with some western political movements such as the Sagebrush Rebellion? Or does Dana Gioia have a point when he notes in his discussion of popular poetry that one faction of critics "characteristically views popular poetry ideologically as an expression of democratic revolutionary, or marginalized class consciousness."[28] It is worth mentioning that agriculture presently involves less than 3% of the American workforce, a minority group by anyone's standards.

What about the persona of the cowboy poet? How do the practitioners, the men and women who write and recite cowboy poetry, see themselves? A few, like Baxter Black or Waddie Mitchell, have made the transition from rancher-veterinarian or cow boss to professional cowboy poet. And, as professional entertainers, they are immersed in a world of performance schedules, book deals, audio tape and cd contracts. However, most of the regulars at the Gathering have heeded the country advice, "Don't give up your day job," and, in my opinion, are most likely to identify themselves in three ways: as being from a particular region in the West; by their specific occupations within the livestock industry; and, most importantly, as cowboy or rancher. One of the best cowboy poets, Joel Nelson, from Alpine, Texas, exemplifies this strong affiliation in his remarks for the 1986 program:

> I have a bachelor's degree in forestry and range management and a year in graduate school in my past . . . . But my education has been picked up on the ranches where I've worked . . . . I've received a good

education every place I ever worked and I've been fortunate in work-
ing on some good outfits with good men . . . . I don't even hope to be
anything but a cowboy. To me, that's the ultimate. My family is happy
with that and all the men I admire are "just cowboys."

Identification with place is strong in the cowboy culture, a culture
richly varied from locale to locale. However, whether a Hispanic cow-
boy poet from West Texas, an Indian cowboy from eastern Montana, or
a woman rancher from a remote corner of Nevada, most cowboy poets
view themselves as keepers of the flame, practicing an art form or a tra-
dition that helps, in some measure, to preserve and perpetuate a way of
life—even as much of the poetry mourns its passing. In his keynote
address for the 1990 Cowboy Poetry Gathering, Wallace McRae said,
"We live and work in the last best place. We poets continue to value the
inspiration and positive reinforcement that we get from the Gathering
being a sharing rather than a competition. Let's hope that some things
never change."[29]
What threatens cowboy poetry most is the increasingly urban audi-
ence and the fact that popularity brings the pressures of conformity.
From the beginning, cowboy poets have had to deal with the bias that
made "cowboy" and "poet," to use Gioia's word, "oxymoronic." Writing
in 1990 about "real" cowboys who "annually gather in Elko, Nevada, to
read their poems to one another," the late Wallace Stegner noted the
public pressure to make Westerners fit into stereotypes:

> Their trouble is that if they write with honesty about exploitation,
> insecurity, hard work, injuries and cows, none of which make even a
> walk-on appearance in *The Virginian* and most of the horse operas it
> has spawned, they will find a smaller and less-enthusiastic audience
> than if they had written about crooked sheriffs and six-guns".

The cliched images still exist. For example, whenever I show the *Cow-
boy Poets* documentary in my literature class, students often respond with
stereotypes of their own. After a recent viewing, one female student said,
"I find it interesting that these macho Marlboro men of the West find
time and enjoy creating poetry. It just does not seem likely that tending
cows and writing poetry would go together well." A young linebacker

on the college football team wrote: "When I think of cowboys I think of Clint Eastwood shooting everybody, not a clean-shaven man reciting poetry." And a bright re-entry student commented, "I can't believe a cowboy would actually write a poem!"

Writing to an audience, as Wallace McRae says, "to get across the way we feel," is one thing. To fall victim to the myths and stereotypes of that audience is another. I see this with the issue of gender and cowboy poetry. Hal Cannon has an interesting perspective on ethnicity that holds true, to a certain extent, for gender:

> Cowboys are generally stereotyped, thanks to Hollywood, as exclusively Anglo-American, yet the truth is that this occupational group has always consisted of a varied mix of ethnic backgrounds. The cowboy's work is so charged with cultural elements that it pervades the life of anyone who participates in it. With its own creed, dress, fancy gear, language, poetry and songs, it often outwardly replaces ethnicity altogether.[30]

I remember at the 1997 Gathering, during a session on women and cowboy poetry, an articulate urban woman wondering aloud: "Where are the women's voices?" They were there. I'm not sure she was hearing them. That gender and ethnicity could be subordinated to occupation is not an easy concept for many outsiders to accept.

At this point in our inquiry into the nature of cowboy poetry and where it belongs, one question remains: is it any good? What have the literary critics had to say? Gioia notes the following:

> While the new popular poetry has received immense coverage from the electronic media and general press, it has garnered relatively little attention from intellectuals and virtually none from established poetry critics. One can understand the reluctance of academic critics. If they have noticed the new popular poetry at all, they immediately see how little it has in common with the kinds of poetry they have been trained to consider worthy of study.[31]

He continues, "Genuinely new artistic developments—be they the revival of popular poetry or the reemergence of form—tend to move dialectically from the margins of established culture rather than smoothly from the central consensus.[32] He is more interested in the phenomenon of cowboy poetry than merits of individual poems. As a matter of fact, he thinks that "individually considered as works of literary art, most of the new popular poetry is undistinguished or worse."[33]

Much of cowboy poetry does have an insider's feel to it. Not everyone responds to a poem about a cow with a prolapsed uterus. Not everyone finds the charm in the "lingo of our calling" as Wallace McRae describes the "purt nears" and "aint's," the references to "kack" and "hackamore." For some, end rhymes are not musical but monotonous. However, in spite of the external pressures to be understood and the pressures of popularity, "Cowboys write for cowboys, not for critics," as cowboy poetry scholar Guy Logsdon observes.[34]

I've listened to hours and hours of cowboy poetry over the years, live and on audiotapes. What would I say about the quality of the poems? That it varies wildly. I particularly like poems about the range, about everyday life, and the poems that celebrate a particular set of values. I've heard some awful poems in each of these categories. The poems of everyday life are often humorous, sometimes scatological, sometimes misogynistic, often echoing themes and motifs at least as old as "The Canterbury Tales." In any of the categories the poems can be sentimental, corny, close-minded. At their best, the poems are ". . . music — a determined, persuasive, reliable, enthusiastic, and crafted music," as Pulitzer poet Mary Oliver defines a poem. At their best, the poems are rich in detail, complex and subtle in their formal elements, and metaphysical truths are revealed in the commonplace.

So, where does cowboy poetry belong? Baxter Black may be right when he says that "Cowboy poetry is someplace between good taste and throwing up in your hat." Kim Stafford has a more eloquent response when he says, "Poetry can serve any cause, but at its best it speaks out of a working life, and tells the worth of the individual, the abundance and wonder of creation, and the politics of the range in the terms of that working life alone."[35] For my own part, I thought of cowboy poetry when I first read this definition by Robert Frost: "Poetry is a way of remembering what it would impoverish us to forget."

Time will tell. For me, the experience of cowboy poetry changed the way I teach literature. After returning to my college classroom from the 1986 Cowboy Poetry Gathering, I started giving students an extra credit assignment: a hundred points for a hundred lines of memorized poetry. Now, after more than a decade of "having been there" that last, often below-zero weekend in January at the Cowboy Poetry Gathering in Elko, I am committed to the virtues of recitation. Now I end "Intro to Lit" with a performance. We discuss the poems the students have chosen from the text, looking at rhyme, meter, symbols, imagery—all the usual. The students rehearse in front of one another. On the last day of class we give a performance. By the time they stand to recite "Lady Lazarus" or "The Road Not Taken" or "We Real Cool," many students have memorized "their" poems. It took a thousand mile trip to get it: poetry is meant to be spoken, seen, and heard. And the best poems are the ones you know by heart.

NOTES

[1] Gioia, Dana."Poetry at the End of Print Culture." Unpublished manuscript. Gioia first presented this critical essay as a guest lecturer at NYU. He has also delivered it at Chapel Hill, Lyons College, University of Galway, and several other schools.

[2] Ibid.

[3] Ibid.

[4] Qtd. in 1995 Cowboy Poetry Gathering program. Programs from 1995 to the present can be found in the Western Folklife Center Archives: 501 Railroad Street / Elko, Nevada 89801 / 702-738-7508 / http://www.westfolk.org

[5] The documentary video "Cowboy Poets" can be found in the Western Folklife Center Archives.

[6] All quoted biographical information on cowboy poet presenters comes from the 1986 or 1990 Cowboy Poetry Gathering programs.

[7] McRae, Wallace. "Some Things Never Change." 1995 Cowboy Poetry Gathering program, 2.

[8] Qtd. in 1997 Cowboy Poetry Gathering program, 32.

[9] Griffith, Jim. "Cowboy Poetry—The First Hundred Years." 1995 Cowboy Poetry Gathering program, 6.

[10] Ibid.

[11] Ibid., 7.

[12] Cannon, Hal. "Cowboy Poets and the Modern World." 1985 Cowboy Poetry Gathering program, 4.

[13] Ibid.

[14] Gioia, Dana. "Poetry at the End of Print Culture," 7.

[15] Ibid., 8.

[16] Ibid., 5.

[17] Ibid., 20

[18] Ibid.

[19] Ibid., 8.

[20] Ibid., 9

[21] Ibid., 13

[22] Respected "literary" poet Jane Hirschfield alluded to pre-classical Greece in reference to the function of poetry at a recent poetry reading Mendocino College at Ukiah, California, September 11, 1998.

[23] Korn, Mike. "Cowboy Poetry: Drawing the Line." 1986 Cowboy Poetry Gathering program, 5.

[24] The appearance in recent years of professor Clay Jenkinson, from, University of Nevada, Reno, reinforces the thematic connection between cowboy poetry and the poetry of classical antiquity. Professor Jenkinson presents a Chautauqua-style program, "Thomas Jefferson and Pastoral Poets," in which he and cowboy poets present the works of pastoral writers such as Horace and Theocritus.

[25] I see a similarity between this excerpt from Tolstoy's *What Is Art?* and Preston's claim for the social usefulness of cowboy poetry: "The task of art is enormous. Through the influence of real art, aided by science, guided by religion, that peaceful co-operation of man which is now maintained by external means . . . by our law courts, police, charitable institutions, factory inspection, and so forth — should be obtained by man's free and joyous activity. Art should cause violence to be set aside."

[26] Preston, Scott. "Cowboy Poetry, Honest American Poetry." 1995 Cowboy Poetry Gathering program, 5.

[27] Cannon, Hal. "Cowboy Poets and the Modern World." 1985 Cowboy Poetry Gathering program, 4.

[28] Gioia, Dana. "Poetry at the End of Print Culture," 7.

[29] McRae, Wallace. "Some Things Never Change." 1995 Cowboy Poetry Gathering program, 3.

[30] Cannon, Hal. "'They ain't very much I would change.' The Life of Curley Fletcher." 1990 Cowboy Poetry Gathering program, 6.

[31] Gioia, Dana. "Poetry at the End of Print Culture," 7.

[32] Ibid., 34.

[33] Ibid., 5.

[34] Logsdon, Guy. "The Qualities of Cowboy Poetry." Keynote address. 1988 Cowboy Poetry Gathering, audiotape, Western Folklife Center Archives.

[35] Stafford, Kim. "How You Came By What You Got." 1995 Cowboy Poetry Gathering program, 11.

WORKS CITED

Egan, Timothy. "The Rape of the West." *The New York Times Book Review*. 6 Sept. 1998:5-6.

Jones, Peter V. *Homer's Odyssey: A Companion to the Translation of Richmond Lattimore*. Carbondale: Southern Illinois University, 1988.

Kennedy, X.J. and Dana Gioia. *An Introduction to Poetry*, 9th ed. New York: Longman, 1998.

Oliver, Mary. *Rules for the Dance: A Handbook for Writing and Reading Metrical Verse*. New York: Houghton Mifflin, 1998.

Ong, Walter. *Orality and Literacy. The Technologizing of the Word*. London: Routledge, 1982.

Stegner, Wallace."The New Literary Frontier." *San Francisco Examiner*. 5 August 1990.

Widmark, Ann. *Poets of the Cowboy West*. New York: Norton, 1995.

WORKS CONSULTED

Bate, Walter Jackson. *Prefaces to Criticism*. New York: Doubleday, 1959.

Cannon, Hal. ed. *Cowboy Poetry*. Salt Lake City: Peregrine Smith Books, 1985.

Gioia, Dana. *Can Poetry Matter? Essays on Poetry and American Culture*. St. Paul: Greywolf Press, 1992.

"Notes Toward a New Bohemia." Grantmakers in the Arts. 5.4., 1994.

Rubin, David C. *Memory in Oral Traditions*. New York: Oxford, 1995.

CAN POETRY MATTER?

American poetry now belongs to a subculture. No longer part of the mainstream of artistic and intellectual life, it has become the specialized occupation of a relatively small and isolated group. Little of the frenetic activity it generates ever reaches outside that closed group. As a class, poets are not without cultural status. Like priests in a town of agnostics, they still command a certain residual prestige. But as individual artists they are almost invisible.

What makes the situation of contemporary poetry particularly surprising is that it comes at a moment of unprecedented expansion for the art. There have never before been so many new books of poetry published, so many anthologies or literary magazines. Never has it been so easy to earn a living as a poet. There are now several thousand college-level jobs in teaching creative writing, and many more at the primary and secondary levels. Congress has even instituted the position of Poet Laureate, as have twenty-five states. One also finds a complex network of public subvention for poets, funded by federal, state, and local agencies, augmented by private support in the form of foundation fellowships, prizes, and subsidized retreats. There has also never before been so much published criticism about contemporary poetry; it fills dozens of literary newsletters and scholarly journals.

The proliferation of new poetry and poetry programs is astounding by any historical measure. Just under a thousand new collections of verse are published each year, in addition to a myriad of new poems printed in magazines both small and large. No one knows how many poetry readings take place each year, but surely the total must run into the tens of thousands. And there are now about 200 graduate creative-writing programs in the United States, and more than a thousand undergraduate ones. With an average of ten poetry students in each graduate section, these programs alone will produce about 20,000 accredited professional poets over the next decade. From such statistics an observer might easily conclude that we live in the golden age of American poetry.

But the poetry boom has been a distressingly confined phenomenon. Decades of public and private funding have created a large professional class for the production and reception of new poetry, comprising legions of teachers, graduate students, editors, publishers, and administrators. Based mostly in universities, these groups have gradually become the primary audience for contemporary verse. Consequently, the energy of

American poetry, which was once directed outward, is now increasingly focused inward. Reputations are made and rewards distributed within the poetry subculture. To adapt Russell Jacoby's definition of contemporary academic renown from *The Last Intellectuals*, a "famous" poet now means someone famous only to other poets. But there are enough poets to make that local fame relatively meaningful. Not long ago, "only poets read poetry" was meant as damning criticism. Now it is a proven marketing strategy.

The situation has become a paradox, a Zen riddle of cultural sociology. Over the past half-century, as American poetry's specialist audience has steadily expanded, its general readership has declined. Moreover, the engines that have driven poetry's institutional success—the explosion of academic writing programs, the proliferation of subsidized magazines and presses, the emergence of a creative-writing career track, and the migration of American literary culture to the university—have unwittingly contributed to its disappearance from public view.

To the average reader, the proposition that poetry's audience has declined may seem self-evident. It is symptomatic of the art's current isolation that within the subculture such notions are often rejected. Like chamber-of-commerce representatives from Parnassus, poetry boosters offer impressive recitations of the numerical growth of publications, programs, and professorships. Given the bullish statistics on poetry's material expansion, how does one demonstrate that its intellectual and spiritual influence has eroded? One cannot easily marshal numbers, but to any candid observer the evidence throughout the world of ideas and letters seems inescapable.

Daily newspapers no longer review poetry. There is, in fact, little coverage of poetry or poets in the general press. From 1984 until this year the National Book Awards dropped poetry as a category. Leading critics rarely review it. In fact, virtually no one reviews it except other poets. Almost no popular collections of contemporary poetry are available except those, like the *Norton Anthology*, targeting an academic audience. It seems, in short, as if the large audience that still exists for quality fiction hardly notices poetry. A reader familiar with the novels of Joyce Carol Oates, John Updike, or John Barth may not even recognize the names of Gwendolyn Brooks, Gary Snyder, or W. D. Snodgrass.

One can see a microcosm of poetry's current position by studying its coverage in the *New York Times*. Virtually never reviewed in the daily edition, new poetry is intermittently discussed in the Sunday *Book Review*, but almost always in group reviews where three books are briefly considered together. Whereas a new novel or biography is reviewed on or around its publication date, a new collection by an important poet like Donald Hall or David Ignatow might wait up to a year for a notice. Or it might never be reviewed at all. Henry Taylor's *The Flying Change* was reviewed only after it had won the Pulitzer Prize. Rodney Jones's *Transparent Gestures* was reviewed months after it had won the National Book Critics Circle Award. Rita Dove's Pulitzer Prize-winning *Thomas and Beulah* was not reviewed by the *Times* at all.

Poetry reviewing is no better anywhere else, and generally it is much worse. The *New York Times* only reflects the opinion that although there is a great deal of poetry around, none of it matters very much to readers, publishers, or advertisers—to anyone, that is, except other poets. For most newspapers and magazines, poetry has become a literary commodity intended less to be read than to be noted with approval. Most editors run poems and poetry reviews the way a prosperous Montana rancher might keep a few buffalo around—not to eat the endangered creatures but to display them for tradition's sake.

Arguments about the decline of poetry's cultural importance are not new. In American letters they date back to the nineteenth century. But the modern debate might be said to have begun in 1934, when Edmund Wilson published the first version of his controversial essay "Is Verse a Dying Technique?" Surveying literary history, Wilson noted that verse's role had grown increasingly narrow since the eighteenth century. In particular, Romanticism's emphasis on intensity made poetry seem so "fleeting and quintessential" that eventually it dwindled into a mainly lyric medium. As verse—which had previously been a popular medium for narrative, satire, drama, even history and scientific speculation—retreated into lyric, prose usurped much of its cultural territory. Truly ambitious writers eventually had no choice but to write in prose. The future of great literature, Wilson speculated, belonged almost entirely to prose.

Wilson was a capable analyst of literary trends. His skeptical assessment of poetry's place in modern letters has been frequently attacked and qualified over the past half century, but it has never been convincingly dismissed. His argument set the ground rules for all subsequent defenders of contemporary poetry. It also provided the starting point for later iconoclasts, such as Delmore Schwartz, Leslie Fiedler, and Christopher Clausen. The most recent and celebrated of these revisionists is Joseph Epstein, whose mordant 1988 critique "Who Killed Poetry?" first appeared in *Commentary* and was reprinted in an extravagantly acrimonious symposium in *AWP Chronicle* (the journal of the Associated Writing Programs). Not so incidentally, Epstein's title pays a double homage to Wilson's essay—first by mimicking the interrogative form of the original title, second by employing its metaphor of death.

Epstein essentially updated Wilson's argument, but with important differences. Whereas Wilson looked on the decline of poetry's cultural position as a gradual process spanning three centuries, Epstein focused on the past few decades. He contrasted the major achievements of the Modernists—the generation of Eliot and Stevens, which led poetry from moribund Romanticism into the twentieth century—with what he felt were the minor accomplishments of the present practitioners. The Modernists, Epstein maintained, were artists who worked from a broad cultural vision. Contemporary writers were "poetry professionals," who operated within the closed world of the university. Wilson blamed poetry's plight on historical forces; Epstein indicted the poets themselves and the institutions they had helped create, especially creative-writing programs. A brilliant polemicist, Epstein intended his essay to be incendiary, and it did ignite an explosion of criticism. No recent essay on American poetry has generated so many immediate responses in literary journals. And certainly none has drawn so much violently negative criticism from poets themselves. To date at least thirty writers have responded in print. Henry Taylor published two rebuttals.

Poets are justifiably sensitive to arguments that poetry has declined in cultural importance, because journalists and reviewers have used such arguments simplistically to declare all contemporary verse irrelevant. Usually the less a critic knows about verse the more readily he or she dismisses it. It is no coincidence, I think, that the two most persuasive essays on poetry's presumed demise were written by outstanding critics of fiction, neither of whom has written extensively about contemporary poetry. It is too soon to judge the accuracy of Epstein's essay, but a literary historian would find Wilson's timing ironic. As Wilson finished his famous essay, Robert Frost, Wallace Stevens, T. S. Eliot, Ezra Pound, Marianne Moore, E. E. Cummings, Robinson Jeffers, H. D. (Hilda Doolittle), Robert Graves, W. H. Auden, Archibald MacLeish, Basil Bunting, and others were writing some of their finest poems, which encompassing history, politics, economics, religion, and philosophy, are among the most culturally inclusive in the history of the language. At the same time, a new generation, which would include Robert Lowell, Elizabeth Bishop, Philip Larkin, Randall Jarrell, Dylan Thomas, A. D. Hope, and others, was just breaking into print. Wilson himself later admitted that the emergence of a versatile and ambitious poet like Auden contradicted several points of his argument. But if Wilson's prophecies were sometimes inaccurate, his sense of poetry's overall situation was depressingly astute. Even if great poetry continues to be written, it has retreated from the center of literary life. Though supported by a loyal coterie, poetry has lost the confidence that it speaks to and for the general culture.

One sees evidence of poetry's diminished stature even within the thriving subculture. The established rituals of the poetry world—the readings, small magazines, workshops, and conferences—exhibit a surprising number of self-imposed limitations. Why, for example, does poetry mix so seldom with music, dance, or theater? At most readings the program consists of verse only—and usually only verse by that night's author. Forty years ago, when Dylan Thomas read, he spent half the program reciting other poets' work. Hardly a self-effacing man, he was nevertheless humble before his art. Today most readings are celebrations less of poetry than of the author's ego. No wonder the audience for such events usually consists entirely of poets, would-be poets, and friends of the author.

Several dozen journals now exist that print only verse. They don't publish literary reviews, just page after page of freshly minted poems. The heart sinks to see so many poems crammed so tightly together, like downcast immigrants in steerage. One can easily miss a radiant poem amid the many lackluster ones. It takes tremendous effort to read these small magazines with openness and attention. Few people bother, generally not even the magazines' contributors. The indifference to poetry in the mass media has created a monster of the opposite kind—journals that love poetry not wisely but too well.

Until about thirty years ago most poetry appeared in magazines that addressed a nonspecialist audience on a range of subjects. Poetry vied for the reader's interest along with political journalism, humor, fiction, and reviews—a competition that proved healthy for all the genres. A poem that didn't command the reader's attention wasn't considered much of a poem. Editors chose verse that they felt would appeal to their particular audiences, and the diversity of magazines assured that a variety of poetry appeared. The early *Kenyon Review* published Robert Lowell's poems next to critical essays and literary reviews. The old *New Yorker* showcased Ogden Nash between cartoons and short stories.

A few general-interest magazines, such as the *New Republic* and the *New Yorker*, still publish poetry in every issue, but, significantly, none except the *Nation* still reviews it regularly. Some poetry appears in the handful of small magazines and quarterlies that consistently discuss a broad cultural agenda with nonspecialist readers, such as the *Threepenny Review*, the *New Criterion*, and the *Hudson Review*. But most poetry is published in journals that address an insular audience of literary professionals, mainly teachers of creative writing and their students. A few of these, such as *American Poetry Review* and *AWP Chronicle*, have moderately large circulations. Many more have negligible readerships. But size is not the problem. The problem is their complacency or resignation about existing only in and for a subculture.

What are the characteristics of a poetry-subculture publication? First, the one subject it addresses is current American literature (supplemented perhaps by a few translations of poets who have already been widely translated). Second, if it prints anything other than poetry, that is usually short fiction. Third, if it runs discursive prose, the essays and reviews are overwhelmingly positive. If it publishes an interview, the tone will be unabashedly reverent toward the author. For these journals critical prose exists not to provide a disinterested perspective on new books but to publicize them. Quite often there are manifest personal connections between the reviewers and the authors they discuss. If occasionally a negative review is published, it will be openly sectarian, rejecting an aesthetic that the magazine has already condemned. The unspoken editorial rule seems to be, "Never surprise or annoy the readers; they are, after all, mainly our friends and colleagues."

By abandoning the hard work of evaluation, the poetry subculture demeans its own art. Since there are too many new poetry collections appearing each year for anyone to evaluate, the reader must rely on the candor and discernment of reviewers to recommend the best books. But the general press has largely abandoned this task, and the specialized press has grown so overprotective of poetry that it is reluctant to make harsh judgments. In his book *American Poetry: Wildness and Domesticity*, Robert Bly has accurately described the corrosive effect of this critical boosterism:

We have an odd situation: although more bad poetry is being published now than ever before in American history, most of the reviews are positive. Critics say, "I never attack what is bad, all that will take care of itself," . . . but the country is full of young poets and readers who are confused by seeing mediocre poetry praised, or never attacked, and who end up doubting their own critical perceptions.

A clubby feeling also typifies most recent anthologies of contemporary poetry. Although these collections represent themselves as trustworthy guides to the best new poetry, they are not compiled for readers outside the academy. More than one editor has discovered that the best way to get an anthology assigned is to include work by the poets who teach the courses. Compiled in the spirit of congenial opportunism, many of these anthologies give the impression that literary quality is a concept that neither an editor nor a reader should take too seriously.

The 1985 *Morrow Anthology of Younger American Poets*, for example, is not so much a selective literary collection as a comprehensive directory of creative-writing teachers (it even offers a photo of each author). Running nearly 800 pages, the volume presents no fewer than 104 important young poets, virtually all of whom teach creative writing. The editorial principle governing selection seems to have been the fear of leaving out some influential colleague. The book does contain a few strong and original poems, but they are surrounded by so many undistinguished exercises that one wonders if the good work got there by design or simply by random sampling. In the drearier patches one suspects that perhaps the book was never truly meant to be read, only assigned.

And that is the real issue. The poetry subculture no longer assumes that all published poems will be read. Like their colleagues in other academic departments, poetry professionals must publish, for purposes of both job security and career advancement. The more they publish, the faster they progress. If they do not publish, or wait too long, their economic futures are in grave jeopardy.

In art, of course, everyone agrees that quality and not quantity matters. Some authors survive on the basis of a single unforgettable poem — Edmund Waller's "Go, lovely rose," for example, or Edwin Markham's "The Man With the Hoe," which was made famous by being reprinted in hundreds of newspapers — an unthinkable occurrence today. But bureaucracies, by their very nature, have difficulty measuring something as intangible as literary quality. When institutions evaluate creative artists for employment or promotion, they still must find some seemingly objective means to do so. As the critic Bruce Bawer has observed,

> A poem is, after all, a fragile thing, and its intrinsic worth, or lack thereof, is a frighteningly subjective consideration; but fellowships, grants, degrees, appointments, and publications are objective facts. They are quantifiable; they can be listed on a résumé.

Poets serious about making careers in institutions understand that the criteria for success are primarily quantitative. They must publish as much as possible as quickly as possible. The slow maturation of genuine creativity looks like laziness to a committee. Wallace Stevens was forty-three when his first book appeared. Robert Frost was thirty-nine. Today these sluggards would be unemployable.

The proliferation of literary journals and presses over the past thirty years has been a response less to an increased appetite for poetry among the public than to the desperate need of writing teachers for professional validation. Like subsidized farming that grows food no one wants, a poetry industry has been created to serve the interests of the producers and not the consumers. And in the process the integrity of the art has been betrayed. Of course, no poet is allowed to admit this in public. The cultural credibility of the professional poetry establishment depends on maintaining a polite hypocrisy. Millions of dollars in public and private funding are at stake. Luckily, no one outside the subculture cares enough to press the point very far. No Woodward and Bernstein will ever investigate a cover-up by members of the Associated Writing Programs.

The new poet makes a living not by publishing literary work but by providing specialized educational services. Most likely he or she either works for or aspires to work for a large institution — usually a state-run enterprise, such as a school district, a college, or a university (or lately even a hospital or prison) — teaching others how to write poetry or, at the highest levels, how to teach others how to write poetry.

To look at the issue in strictly economic terms, most contemporary poets have been alienated from their original cultural function. As Marx maintained and few economists have disputed, changes in a class's economic function eventually transform its values and behavior. In poetry's case, the socioeconomic changes have led to a divided literary culture:

the superabundance of poetry within a small class and the impoverish-ment outside it. One might even say that outside the classroom—where society demands that the two groups interact—poets and the common reader are no longer on speaking terms.

The divorce of poetry from the educated reader has had another, more pernicious result. Seeing so much mediocre verse not only published but praised, slogging through so many dull anthologies and small magazines, most readers—even sophisticated ones like Joseph Epstein—now as-sume that no significant new poetry is being written. This public skepti-cism represents the final isolation of verse as an art form in contempo-rary society.

The irony is that this skepticism comes in a period of genuine achieve-ment. Gresham's Law, that bad coinage drives out good, only half ap-plies to current poetry. The sheer mass of mediocrity may have fright-ened away most readers, but it has not yet driven talented writers from the field. Anyone patient enough to weed through the tangle of contem-porary work finds an impressive and diverse range of new poetry. Adrienne Rich, for example, despite her often overbearing polemics, is a major poet by any standard. The best work of Donald Justice, Anthony Hecht, Donald Hall, James Merrill, Louis Simpson, William Stafford, and Richard Wilbur—to mention only writers of the older generation— can hold its own against anything in the national literature. One might also add Sylvia Plath and James Wright, two strong poets of the same generation who died early. America is also a country rich in émigré po-etry, as major writers like Czeslaw Milosz, Nina Cassian, Derek Walcott, Joseph Brodsky, and Thom Gunn demonstrate.

Without a role in the broader culture, however, talented poets lack the confidence to create public speech. Occasionally a writer links up rewardingly to a social or political movement. Rich, for example, has used feminism to expand the vision of her work. Robert Bly wrote his finest poetry to protest the Vietnam War. His sense of addressing a large and diverse audience added humor, breadth, and humanity to his previ-ously minimalist verse. But it is a difficult task to marry the Muse hap-pily to politics. Consequently, most contemporary poets, knowing that they are virtually invisible in the larger culture, focus on the more inti-mate forms of lyric and meditative verse. (And a few loners, like X. J. Kennedy and John Updike, turn their genius to the critically disrepu-table demimonde of light verse and children's poetry.) Therefore, although current American poetry has not often excelled in public forms like po-litical or satiric verse, it has nonetheless produced personal poems of unsurpassed beauty and power. Despite its manifest excellence, this new work has not found a public beyond the poetry subculture, because the traditional machinery of transmission—the reliable reviewing, honest criticism, and selective anthologies—has broken down. The audience that once made Frost and Eliot, Cummings and Millay, part of its cultural vision remains out of reach. Today Walt Whitman's challenge "To have great poets, there must be great audiences, too" reads like an indictment. To maintain their activities, subcultures usually require institutions, since the general society does not share their interests. Nudists flock to "nature camps" to express their unfettered lifestyle. Monks remain in monasteries to protect their austere ideals. As long as poets belonged to a broader class of artists and intellectuals, they centered their lives in urban bohemias, where they maintained a distrustful independence from institutions. Once poets began moving into universities, they abandoned the working-class heterogeneity of Greenwich Village and North Beach for the professional homogeneity of academia.

At first they existed on the fringes of English departments, which was probably healthy. Without advanced degrees or formal career paths, poets were recognized as special creatures. They were allowed—like aboriginal chieftains visiting an anthropologist's campsite—to behave according to their own laws. But as the demand for creative writing grew, the poet's job expanded from merely literary to administrative duties. At the university's urging, these self-trained writers designed history's first institutional curricula for young poets. Creative writing evolved from occasional courses taught within the English department into its own undergraduate major or graduate-degree program. Writers fashioned their academic specialty in the image of other university studies. As the new writing departments multiplied, the new professionals patterned their infrastructure—job titles, journals, annual conventions, organizations— according to the standards not of urban bohemia but of educational institutions. Out of the professional networks this educational expansion created, the subculture of poetry was born.

Initially, the multiplication of creative-writing programs must have been a dizzyingly happy affair. Poets who had scraped by in bohemia or had spent their early adulthood fighting the Second World War suddenly secured stable, well-paying jobs. Writers who had never earned much public attention found themselves surrounded by eager students. Poets who had been too poor to travel flew from campus to campus and from conference to conference, to speak before audiences of their peers. As Wilfrid Sheed once described a moment in John Berryman's career, "Through the burgeoning university network, it was suddenly possible to think of oneself as a national poet, even if the nation turned out to consist entirely of English Departments." The bright postwar world promised a renaissance for American poetry.

In material terms that promise has been fulfilled beyond the dreams of anyone in Berryman's Depression-scarred generation. Poets now occupy niches at every level of academia, from a few sumptuously endowed chairs with six-figure salaries to the more numerous part-time stints that pay roughly the same as Burger King. But even at minimum wage, teaching poetry earns more than writing it ever did. Before the creative-writing boom, being a poet usually meant living in genteel poverty or worse. While the sacrifices poetry demanded caused much individual suffering, the rigors of serving Milton's "thankless Muse" also delivered the collective cultural benefit of frightening away all but committed artists.

Today poetry is a modestly upwardly mobile, middle-class profession — not as lucrative as waste management or dermatology but several big steps above the squalor of bohemia. Only a philistine would romanticize the blissfully banished artistic poverty of yesteryear. But a clear-eyed observer must also recognize that by opening the poet's trade to all applicants and by employing writers to do something other than write, institutions have changed the social and economic identity of the poet from artist to educator. In social terms the identification of poet with teacher is now complete. The first question one poet now asks another upon being introduced is "Where do you teach?" The problem is not that poets teach. The campus is not a bad place for a poet to work. It's just a bad place for *all* poets to work. Society suffers by losing the imagination and vitality that poets brought to public culture. Poetry suffers when literary standards are forced to conform to institutional ones.

Even within the university contemporary poetry now exists as a subculture. The teaching poet finds that he or she has little in common with academic colleagues. The academic study of literature over the past twenty-five years has veered off in a theoretical direction with which most imaginative writers have little sympathy or familiarity. Thirty years ago detractors of creative-writing programs predicted that poets in universities would become enmeshed in literary criticism and scholarship.

This prophecy has proved spectacularly wrong. Poets have created enclaves in the academy. Pressed to keep up with the plethora of new poetry, small magazines, professional journals, and anthologies, they are frequently also less well read in the literature of the past. Their peers in the English department generally read less contemporary poetry and more literary theory. In many departments writers and literary theorists are openly at war. Bringing the two groups under one roof has paradoxically made each more territorial. Isolated even within the university, the poet, whose true subject is the whole of human existence, has reluctantly become an educational specialist.

To understand how radically the social situation of the American poet has changed, one need only compare today with fifty years ago. In 1940, with the notable exception of Robert Frost, few poets were working in colleges unless, like Mark Van Doren and Yvor Winters, they taught traditional academic subjects. The only creative-writing program was an experiment begun a few years earlier at the University of Iowa. The Modernists exemplified the options that poets had for making a living. They could enter middle-class professions, as had T. S. Eliot (a banker turned publisher), Wallace Stevens (a corporate insurance lawyer), and William Carlos Williams (a pediatrician). Or they could live in bohemia supporting themselves as artists, as, in different ways, did Ezra Pound, E. E. Cummings, and Marianne Moore. If the city proved unattractive, they could, like Robinson Jeffers, scrape by in a rural arts colony like Carmel, California. Or they might become farmers, like the young Robert Frost.

Most often poets supported themselves as editors or reviewers, actively taking part in the artistic and intellectual life of their time. Archibald MacLeish was an editor and writer at *Fortune*. James Agee reviewed movies for *Time* and the *Nation,* and eventually wrote screenplays for Hollywood. Randall Jarrell reviewed books. Weldon Kees wrote about jazz and modern art. Delmore Schwartz reviewed everything. Even poets who eventually took up academic careers spent intellectually broadening apprenticeships in literary journalism. The young Robert Hayden covered music and theater for Michigan's black press. R. P. Blackmur, who never completed high school, reviewed books for *Hound & Horn* before teaching at Princeton. Occasionally a poet might supplement his or her income by giving a reading or lecture, but these occasions were rare. Robinson Jeffers, for example, was fifty-four when he gave his first public reading. For most poets, the sustaining medium was not the classroom or the podium but the written word.

If poets supported themselves by writing, it was mainly by writing prose. Paying outlets for poetry were limited. Beyond a few national magazines, which generally preferred light verse or political satire, there were at any one time only a few dozen journals that published a significant amount of poetry. The emergence of a serious new quarterly like *Partisan Review* or *Furioso* was an event of real importance, and a small but dedicated audience eagerly looked forward to each issue. If people could not afford to buy copies, they borrowed them or visited public libraries. As for books of poetry, if one excludes vanity-press editions, fewer than a hundred new titles were published each year. But the books that did appear were reviewed in daily newspapers as well as magazines and quarterlies. A focused monthly like *Poetry* could cover virtually the entire field.

Reviewers fifty years ago were by today's standards extraordinarily tough. They said exactly what they thought, even about their most influential contemporaries. Listen, for example, to Randall Jarrell's description of a book by the famous anthologist Oscar Williams: it "gave the impression of having been written on a typewriter by a typewriter." That remark kept Jarrell out of subsequent Williams anthologies, but he did not hesitate to publish it. Or consider Jarrell's assessment of Archibald MacLeish's public poem "America Was Promises": it "might have been devised by a YMCA secretary at a home for the mentally deficient." Or read Weldon Kees's one-sentence review of Muriel Rukeyser's "Wake Island"—"There's one thing you can say about Muriel: she's not lazy." But these same reviewers could write generously about poets they admired, as Jarrell did about Elizabeth Bishop, and Kees about Wallace Stevens. Their praise mattered, because readers knew it did not come lightly.

The reviewers of fifty years ago knew that their primary loyalty must lie not with their fellow poets or publishers but with the readers. Consequently they reported their reactions with scrupulous honesty, even when their opinions might lose them literary allies and writing assignments. In discussing new poetry they addressed a wide community of educated readers. Without talking down to their audience, they cultivated a public idiom. Prizing clarity and accessibility, they avoided specialist jargon and pedantic displays of scholarship. They also tried, as serious intellectuals should but specialists often do not, to relate what was happening in poetry to social, political, and artistic trends. They charged modern poetry with cultural importance and made it the focal point of their intellectual discourse.

Ill-paid, overworked, and underappreciated, this argumentative group of "practical" critics, all of them poets, accomplished remarkable things. They defined the canon of Modernist poetry, established methods to analyze verse of extraordinary difficulty, and identified the new mid-century generation of American poets (Lowell, Roethke, Bishop, Berryman, and others) that still dominates our literary consciousness. Whatever one thinks of their literary canon or critical principles, one must admire the intellectual energy and sheer determination of these critics, who developed as writers without grants or permanent faculty positions, often while working precariously on free-lance assignments. They represent a high point in American intellectual life. Even fifty years later their names still command more authority than those of all but a few contemporary critics. A short roll call would include John Berryman, R. P. Blackmur, Louise Bogan, John Ciardi, Horace Gregory, Langston Hughes, Randall Jarrell, Weldon Kees, Kenneth Rexroth, Delmore Schwartz, Karl Shapiro, Allen Tate, and Yvor Winters. Although contemporary poetry has its boosters and publicists, it has no group of comparable dedication and talent able to address the general literary community.

Like all genuine intellectuals, these critics were visionary. They believed that if modern poets did not have an audience, they could create one. And gradually they did. It was not a mass audience; few American poets of any period have enjoyed a direct relationship with the general public. It was a cross-section of artists and intellectuals, including scientists, clergymen, educators, lawyers, and, of course, writers. This group constituted a literary intelligentsia, made up mainly of nonspecialists, who took poetry as seriously as fiction and drama. Recently Donald Hall and other critics have questioned the size of this audience by citing the low average sales of a volume of new verse by an established poet during the period (usually under a thousand copies). But these skeptics do not understand how poetry was read then.

America was a smaller, less affluent country in 1940, with about half its current population and one-sixth its current real GNP. In those pre-paperback days of the late Depression neither readers nor libraries could afford to buy as many books as they do today. Nor was there a large captive audience of creative-writing students who bought books of contemporary poetry for classroom use. Readers usually bought poetry in two forms—in an occasional *Collected Poems* by a leading author, or in anthologies. The comprehensive collections of writers like Frost, Eliot, Auden, Jeffers, Wylie, and Millay sold very well, were frequently reprinted, and stayed perpetually in print. (Today most *Collected Poems* disappear after one printing.) Occasionally a book of new poems would capture the public's fancy. Edwin Arlington Robinson's *Tristram* (1927) became a Literary Guild selection. Frost's *A Further Range* sold 50,000 copies as a 1936 Book-of-the-Month Club selection. But people knew poetry mainly from anthologies, which they not only bought but also read, with curiosity and attention.

Louis Untermeyer's *Modern American Poetry*, first published in 1919, was frequently revised to keep it up to date and was a perennial bestseller. My 1942 edition, for example, had been reprinted five times by 1945. My edition of Oscar Williams's *A Pocket Book of Modern Poetry* had been reprinted nineteen times in fourteen years. Untermeyer and Williams prided themselves on keeping their anthologies broad-based and timely. They tried to represent the best of what was being published. Each edition added new poems and poets and dropped older ones. The public appreciated their efforts. Poetry anthologies were an indispensable part of any serious reader's library. Random House's popular Modern Library series, for example, included not one but two anthologies — Selden Rodman's *A New Anthology of Modern Poetry* and Conrad Aiken's *Twentieth-Century American Poetry*. All these collections were read and reread by a diverse public. Favorite poems were memorized. Difficult authors like Eliot and Thomas were actively discussed and debated. Poetry mattered outside the classroom.

Today these general readers constitute the audience that poetry has lost. United by intelligence and curiosity, this heterogeneous group cuts across lines of race, class, age, and occupation. Representing our cultural intelligentsia, they are the people who support the arts — who buy classical and jazz records; who attend foreign films, serious theater, opera, symphony, and dance; who read quality fiction and biographies; who listen to public radio and subscribe to the best journals. (They are also often the parents who read poetry to their children and remember, once upon a time in college or high school or kindergarten, liking it themselves.) No one knows the size of this community, but even if one accepts the conservative estimate that it accounts for only two percent of the U.S. population, it still represents a potential audience of almost five million readers. However healthy poetry may appear within its professional subculture, it has lost this larger audience, who represents poetry's bridge to the general culture.

But why should anyone but a poet care about the problems of American poetry? What possible relevance does this archaic art form have to contemporary society? In a better world, poetry would need no justification beyond the sheer splendor of its own existence. As Wallace Stevens once observed, "The purpose of poetry is to contribute to man's happiness." Children know this essential truth when they ask to hear their favorite nursery rhymes again and again. Aesthetic pleasure needs no justification, because a life without such pleasure is one not worth living.

But the rest of society has mostly forgotten the value of poetry. To the general reader, discussions about the state of poetry sound like the debating of foreign politics by émigrés in a seedy café. Or, as Cyril Connolly more bitterly described it, "Poets arguing about modern poetry: jackals snarling over a dried-up well." Anyone who hopes to broaden poetry's audience—critic, teacher, librarian, poet, or lonely literary amateur—faces a daunting challenge. How does one persuade justly skeptical readers, in terms they can understand and appreciate, that poetry still matters?

A passage in William Carlos Williams's "Asphodel, That Greeny Flower" provides a possible starting point. Written toward the end of the author's life, after he had been partly paralyzed by a stroke, the lines sum up the hard lessons about poetry and audience that Williams had learned over years of dedication to both poetry and medicine. He wrote,

> My heart rouses
> thinking to bring you news
> of something
> that concerns you
> and concerns many men. Look at
> what passes for the new.
> You will not find it there but in
> despised poems.
> It is difficult
> to get the news from poems
> yet men die miserably every day
> for lack
> of what is found there.

Williams understood poetry's human value but had no illusions about the difficulties his contemporaries faced in trying to engage the audience that needed the art most desperately. To regain poetry's readership one must begin by meeting Williams's challenge to find what "concerns many men," not simply what concerns poets.

There are at least two reasons why the situation of poetry matters to the entire intellectual community. The first involves the role of language in a free society. Poetry is the art of using words charged with their utmost meaning. A society whose intellectual leaders lose the skill to shape, appreciate, and understand the power of language will become the slaves of those who retain it—be they politicians, preachers, copywriters, or newscasters. The public responsibility of poetry has been pointed out repeatedly by modern writers. Even the arch-symbolist Stéphane Mallarmé praised the poet's central mission to "purify the words of the tribe." And Ezra Pound warned that

> Good writers are those who keep the language efficient. That is to say, keep it accurate, keep it clear. It doesn't matter whether a good writer wants to be useful or whether the bad writer wants to do harm. . . . If a nation's literature declines, the nation atrophies and decays.

Or, as George Orwell wrote after the Second World War, "One ought to recognize that the present political chaos is connected with the decay of language . . . ." Poetry is not the entire solution to keeping the nation's language clear and honest, but one is hard pressed to imagine a country's citizens improving the health of its language while abandoning poetry.

The second reason why the situation of poetry matters to all intellectuals is that poetry is not alone among the arts in its marginal position. If the audience for poetry has declined into a subculture of specialists, so too have the audiences for most contemporary art forms, from serious drama to jazz. The unprecedented fragmentation of American high culture during the past half-century has left most arts in isolation from one another as well as from the general audience. Contemporary classical music scarcely exists as a living art outside university departments and conservatories. Jazz, which once commanded a broad popular audience, has become the semi-private domain of aficionados and musicians. (Today even influential jazz innovators cannot find places to perform in many metropolitan centers—and for an improvisatory art the inability to perform is a crippling liability.) Much serious drama is now confined to the margins of American theater, where it is seen only by actors, aspiring actors, playwrights, and a few diehard fans. Only the visual arts, perhaps because of their financial glamour and upper-class support, have largely escaped the decline in public attention.

The most serious question for the future of American culture is whether the arts will continue to exist in isolation and decline into subsidized academic specialties or whether some possibility of rapprochement with the educated public remains. Each of the arts must face the challenge separately, and no art faces more towering obstacles than poetry. Given the decline of literacy, the proliferation of other media, the crisis in humanities education, the collapse of critical standards, and the sheer weight of past failures, how can poets possibly succeed in being heard? Wouldn't it take a miracle?

Toward the end of her life Marianne Moore wrote a short poem called "O To Be a Dragon." This poem recalled the biblical dream in which the Lord appeared to King Solomon and said, "Ask what I shall give thee." Solomon wished for a wise and understanding heart. Moore's wish is harder to summarize. Her poem reads,

> If I, like Solomon, . . .
> could have my wish—
>
> my wish—O to be a dragon,
> a symbol of the power of Heaven—of silkworm
> size or immense; at times invisible.
> Felicitous phenomenon!

Moore got her wish. She became, as all genuine poets do, "a symbol of the power of Heaven." She succeeded in what Robert Frost called "the utmost of ambition"—namely, "to lodge a few poems where they will be hard to get rid of." She is permanently part of the "felicitous phenomenon" of American literature.

So wishes can come true—even extravagant ones. If I, like Marianne Moore, could have my wish, and I, like Solomon, could have the self-control not to wish for myself, I would wish that poetry could again become a part of American public culture. I don't think this is impossible. All it would require is that poets and poetry teachers take more responsibility for bringing their art to the public. I will close with six modest proposals for how this dream might come true.

1. *When poets give public readings, they should spend part of every program reciting other people's work—preferably poems they admire by writers they do not know personally.* Readings should be celebrations of poetry in general, not merely of the featured author's work.

2. *When arts administrators plan public readings, they should avoid the standard subculture format of poetry only.* Mix poetry with the other arts, especially music. Plan evenings honoring dead or foreign writers. Combine short critical lectures with poetry performances. Such combinations would attract an audience from beyond the poetry world without compromising quality.

3. *Poets need to write prose about poetry more often, more candidly, and more effectively.* Poets must recapture the attention of the broader intellectual community by writing for nonspecialist publications. They must also avoid the jargon of contemporary academic criticism and write in a public idiom. Finally, poets must regain the reader's trust by candidly admitting what they don't like as well as promoting what they like. Professional courtesy has no place in literary journalism.

4. *Poets who compile anthologies—or even reading lists—should be scrupulously honest in including only poems they genuinely admire.* Anthologies are poetry's gateway to the general culture. They should not be used as pork barrels for the creative-writing trade. An art expands its audience by presenting masterpieces, not mediocrity. Anthologies should be compiled to move, delight, and instruct readers, not to flatter the writing teachers who assign books. Poet-anthologists must never trade the Muse's property for professional favors.

5. *Poetry teachers, especially at the high school and undergraduate levels, should spend less time on analysis and more on performance.* Poetry needs to be liberated from literary criticism. Poems should be memorized, recited, and performed. The sheer joy of the art must be emphasized. The pleasure of performance is what first attracts children to poetry, the sensual excitement of speaking and hearing

the words of the poem. Performance was also the teaching technique that kept poetry vital for centuries. Maybe it also holds the key to poetry's future.

6. *Finally, poets and arts administrators should use radio to expand the art's audience.* Poetry is an aural medium, and thus ideally suited to radio. A little imaginative programming at the hundreds of college and public-supported radio stations could bring poetry to millions of listeners. Some programming exists, but it is stuck mostly in the standard subculture format of living poets reading their own work. Mixing poetry with music on classical and jazz stations or creating innovative talk-radio formats could reestablish a direct relationship between poetry and the general audience.

The history of art tells the same story over and over. As art forms develop, they establish conventions that guide creation, performance, instruction, even analysis. But eventually these conventions grow stale. They begin to stand between the art and its audience. Although much wonderful poetry is being written, the American poetry establishment is locked into a series of exhausted conventions—outmoded ways of presenting, discussing, editing, and teaching poetry. Educational institutions have codified them into a stifling bureaucratic etiquette that enervates the art. These conventions may once have made sense, but today they imprison poetry in an intellectual ghetto.

It is time to experiment, time to leave the well-ordered but stuffy classroom, time to restore a vulgar vitality to poetry and unleash the energy now trapped in the subculture. There is nothing to lose. Society has already told us that poetry is dead. Let's build a funeral pyre out of the desiccated conventions piled around us and watch the ancient, spangle-feathered, unkillable phoenix rise from the ashes.

THE LARIATI VERSUS/VERSES THE LITERATI: LOPING TOWARD DANA GIOIA'S DREAM COME REAL

I grew up in a bookless house—except for a bible stored in its original box high out of reach on a closet shelf, and a copy of *Vein of Iron*, the history of the Pick & Mathers iron ore mining company for whom my father worked. My mother, of course, recited a few nursery rhymes to me when I was young. After kindergarten, however, I have little recollection of the nuns at St. Mary's grade school teaching poetry, aside from Sister Mary Ivan ("The Terrible") sentencing us to memorize and recite in front of class "Paul Revere's Ride"—two lines per violation as punishment. Daniel Bensoni, God bless him wherever he is, sinned his way to a record 80 lines. In much the same way as I went from holy parochial school to hoodlum Hurley High, I fell in one swoop from Mother Goose to poetry-as-penance (say three Our Fathers, three Hail Marys, 30 lines of "Paul Revere's Ride" and go my child and sin no more) to serious study of The Masters in high school literature classes.

In those days, in that isolated neck of the Midwest north woods, Poetry In The Schools programs did not exist. It was easy to make the standard "all-poets-are-dead" deduction. More significantly, I decided that none of the poems that we were forced to decode and decipher were about my life, my interests, my passions. Instead of Grecian urns in our house, we had Red Wing crocks, coal buckets, washtubs, and bushel baskets. Moreover, why were there no poems about hunting ducks, fishing for native brookies, making hard hits on the gridiron, running wild between beer joints on a fast motorcycle? If my life didn't matter to the art of poetry, then why should poetry matter to me? At 16, in the midst of a blue-collar environment, this decision to scratch poetry off my Christmas list forever was that simple.

The influences of the subsequent five years, which transformed poetry from foe to partner-for-life, are too involved to delineate now, but I will pinpoint the single poem most responsible for the complete turnabout: "Zimmer, Drunk and Alone, Dreaming of Old Football Games," by renowned poet and editor, Paul Zimmer. I remember asking my freshman composition instructor, David Steingass (my first living poet!), if

this was in fact a legitimate poem. Not only was Zimmer writing in con-
crete images made from a clear, crisp language that dazzled the eye and
ear on that first jump out of the chute, he was also addressing experi-
ences and emotions that I could relate to. Poetry, like a friendly ghost,
like lightning you could hug without harm, had struck close to home,
and I instantly loved the notion that my tiny life might be worthy of such
power in song and sentiment. Poetry, all of a sudden, made sense and
mattered.

Since the May [1991] issue of *The Atlantic* ran Dana Gioia's essay,
"Can Poetry Matter?" I've received numerous Xeroxes by mail from
both writer and non-writer friends, most of whom praised Gioia's com-
ments/accusations. "CAN Poetry Matter?" The title lures both writers
and readers of poetry (Gioia maintains that they, unfortunately, are one
and the same) to this provocative essay, and in fact, if you haven't al-
ready received your copy, chances are that you soon will—I copied cop-
ies of copies and sent them to friends who wrote back and said they
followed suit. Little could Dana Gioia have known that he was invent-
ing The Chain Essay. And speaking of "suit," are we all in violation of
copyright laws? If so, my apologies to *The Atlantic*. And to their lawyers,
this: my most valuable assets are a 19-year-old buckskin gelding with
heaves (since the initial publication of this piece, ol' Buck died) and a
1971 Chevy Monte Carlo with a flat camshaft (140,000 miles, so far)
and running on six and one-half of its eight cylinders—I "make my liv-
ing" writing and reciting poetry.

I agree, on the whole, with Dana Gioia's thesis that ". . . although
there is a great deal of poetry around, none of it matters very much to
readers, publishers or advertisers—to anyone, that is, except other po-
ets; . . . today most readings (mixing so seldom with music, dance, or
theatre) are celebrations less of poetry than of the poet's ego; . . . outside
the classroom—where society demands that the two groups interact—
poets and the common reader are no longer on speaking terms."

There are, however, exceptions, and cowboy poetry is one of them.
That's right, I said "cowboy poetry"—as in range rhymes and bunk-
house ballads written and recited by buckaroo bards and cowpuncher
poets. Go ahead, chuckle. Better yet, laugh loudly. Cowboy poets wel-
come laughter, which, in the lives of "regular folks," goes hand in hand
with fun. I said chuckle, not snicker. But if the latter comes more spon-
taneously to the Literati elitists among you, first reconsider my thesis: in

the Lariati arena at least three of Gioia's six proposals take root and thrive naturally out of the tradition.

First, cowboy poets "recite other people's works," especially the poems of those who rode/wrote before them. They do so in large part to pay tribute to their legacy and history, and they do so alongside contemporary works to illustrate the continuations and connections in form and focus, as well as the changes, which they deem necessary for the growth of their art. Call it "folk art," if it will make you snicker or squirm any less, but then consider the Texas cowboy poet, Joel Nelson, who often recites Robert Frost's "The Road Not Taken," which, he deems, is about a lot of cowboys he's ridden with over the years. And consider also Rod McQueary from Ruby Valley, Nevada, or Wyoming cowboy poet, Bill Jones, both Viet Nam Vets, who've written and recited strong free verse poems about the war we all suffered through. Good poetry is good poetry—whoever, wherever, etc.—and usually reaches toward the universal. Period.

Cowboy poets also fulfill the second Gioia proposal by "mixing poetry with other arts, especially music, and by planning evenings honoring dead or foreign writers." Thousands of people—mostly non-poets!— pay up to $25 per ticket (sold out months in advance) to these performances, called "Gatherings," in Elko, Nevada, at the end of January, in the bitter middle of winter. The western renaissance began in 1985 with the first Cowboy Poetry Gathering, and since then the number of similar celebrations across the U.S. continues to grow. In April of 1992, I recited cowboy poems in D.C. (it's your guess, District of Columbia or Dodge City?) as part of a show called "Poets, Politicians, & Other Storytellers," sponsored by the National Council for the Traditional Arts and The George Washington University. Back-to-back with a lengthy traditional ballad written in the 1880's, I recited my own rhymed and metered poems right alongside the free verse work. As a grand finale to the show, the Legendary Ray Hicks told his engaging Jack Tales. Like most cowboy poetry gatherings combining musicians, storytellers, a cappella soloists, and theatrical presentations, the latter which often include verse, the D.C. performance offered a variety of forms. The response was enthusiastic, once again proving that audiences of wide variation in sentiment, lifestyle, whatever, have turned out on both coasts to, as my mentor Dick Hugo so often put it, "have fun with the sound of words."

In the fifth entry of his "wishlist sextet," Gioia states that "The sheer joy of the art must be emphasized. The pleasure of performance is what first attracts children to poetry, the sensual excitement of speaking and hearing the words of the poem." I thank my mother for planting this early seed; it wasn't her fault that it took 20 years to germinate. Maybe, had I been lucky enough to have been raised on a ranch out West where I'd heard some old cowpoke say poems around a campfire, I'd have become a fan of the language much sooner.

I remember the first time I heard Richard Hugo perform — not simply read, but perform — his poem "Plans for Altering the River." Dick had the knack for giving sometimes long, but never boring introductions to poems and, though I hung closely to his every word, on this occasion, before I realized it, he was already two or three lines into the poem . . .

> Those who favor our plan to alter the river
> raise your hand. Thank you for your vote.
> Last week, you'll recall. . . .

A bit of fancy footwork? A skosh of showmanship? Surprise! You bet. And why not? Anything to break the cloned reading syndrome ("the title of my next poem is. . . ."). "The only rule," Dick used to say about writing, "is don't be boring." Sweat runneling horizontally across his furrowed brow, he moved back and forth behind the lab desk in the tiered botany lecture hall. And the lines he recited, without a net, surged through me like a double shot of 190 proof Everclear.

And thus, I took it as no mere coincidence years later, after Hugo's death and while I was filling in (I use the phrase loosely) for him at the University of Montana, that it was in the same room where I first heard cowboy poetry recited. And no coincidence either that the poet was Wallace McRae, as highly regarded in the Lariati arena as Dick Hugo was in the Literati world. Both poets are Montana institutions, if not heroes, and now that I closely consider their work side-by-side, their writing harbors very similar sentiments concerning Montana's people and landscapes. And, again, no coincidence whatsoever that years after the death of the man who taught me almost everything I know about poetry, and while I still grieved, Wallace McRae should come along and we would strike up a friendship based in large part on our mutual love for Montana, for the land and the language, the latter which Wallace refers to as "the lingo of our calling."

Cowboy poetry. What would Dick Hugo have thought? Doggerel? Something to be ignored or discounted in English wings of universities everywhere? I think not. Not if he'd witnessed an audience of 3,000 strong acknowledging that people's individual lives—in this case, lives that are often rurally isolated—are significant because of the honest emotion invested into, and expressed out of, those lives. He'd have chuckled (not snickered) with delight, I think, at the definition I've coined for cowboy poetry: "the ring and ricochet of lingo off the stirrup bone (stapes) of the middle ear." The truth be known, Dick was not enamored of horses. But I'd bet my kack (saddle) he'd have loved the language of the horseman—reata, latigo, tapadera, concho, hackamore—much of it derived from the Spanish, "the loving tongue," as Charles Badger Clark referred to it in his cowboy poem, "A Border Affair."

All to say, that maybe—just maybe—the overwhelming enthusiastic response to cowboy poetry, by audiences from many walks of life, is in some part due to a non-academic yearning to fulfill a genuine integral need for verse, a need still alive and kicking/bucking/galloping within most of us, a need to hear aloud emotions and ideas conveyed in that good old form, the one most "jagged on the right." In retrospect, I believe I felt this need even as a 16-year-old renegade resisting most everything that had to do with school. I realized that poetry had little, in fact, to do with scholastics. Rather, it was about living life with passion and awareness—my mission from the get-go—which was why I was stung by poetry's rejection of me.

Obviously, cowboy poetry was not my "savior." (The closest Zimmer came to the subject was a piece titled "Zimmer The Drugstore Cowboy.") Nor am I suggesting that cowboy poetry is the perfect template by which the academic world of verse should be shaped. Failing every bit as miserably, cowboy poetry falls far short of accomplishing the remaining trio of Gioia Wishes:

3. *Poets need to write prose about poetry more often, more candidly, and more effectively.* Poets must recapture the attention of the broader intellectual community by writing for nonspecialist publications. They must also avoid the jargon of contemporary academic criticism and write in a public idiom. Finally, poets must regain the reader's trust by candidly admitting what they don't like as well as promoting what they like. Professional courtesy has no place in literary journalism.

4. Poets who compile anthologies—or even reading lists—should be scrupulously honest in including only poems they genuinely admire. Anthologies are poetry's gateway to the general culture. They should not be used as pork barrels for the creative-writing trade. An art expands its audience by presenting masterpieces, not mediocrity. Anthologies should be compiled to move, delight, and instruct readers, not to flatter the writing teachers who assign books. Poet-anthologists must never trade the Muse's property for professional favors.

6. Finally, poets and arts administrators should use radio to expand the art's audience. Poetry is an aural medium, and thus ideally suited to radio. A little imaginative programming at the hundreds of college and public-supported radio stations could bring poetry to millions of listeners. Some programming exists, but it is stuck mostly in the standard subculture format of living poets reading their own work. Mixing poetry with music on classical and jazz stations or creating innovative talk-radio formats could reestablish a direct relationship between poetry and the general audience.

I simply wish, therefore, to offer a few observations and point out a few connections between the Literati and the Lariati, including two of Gioia's most prominent metaphors, which happen to be rooted in rural landscape, both involving agriculture and one of them, most interestingly, set on my home ground. "Most editors," he proclaims, "run poems and poetry reviews the way a prosperous Montana rancher might keep a few buffalo around—not to eat the endangered creatures but to display them for tradition's sake . . . ." And a few pages later, "Like subsidized farming that grows food no one wants, a poetry industry has been created to serve the interests of the producers and not the consumers."

The Lariati arena has proven to me that "consumers" are out there and anxious to "buy." Perhaps the Literati could cue to the Lariati's successes in attracting these consumers to "market." If ever poetry, especially on any large scale from the academic world, is going to appeal to regular folks, be they cowboys/cowgirls, fishnetters, engineers, farmers, executives, athletes, mill workers, miners, or what have you, the line drawn—with a D-8 bulldozer built by Rolls Royce—between fine art and folk art is going to have to be narrowed a great deal. To that end, maybe we could be more willing to discuss—especially throughout a reading—or even explain the processes, thoughts, emotions, associations that went into the making of a poem. After reciting "Staircase," one of my more involved pieces, in Elko, someone said, "You know, I read that poem in your book several times and I finally decided I didn't like it because it got a little too smoky for me, but your introduction to it tonight made it ring clearer."

Most people expect introductions. The bulk of what they read is journalistic prose, which usually offers a "guiding hand" to lead them into and through the subject matter step by step. Poets, on the contrary, eventually learn that poems tend to begin somewhere in the middle, that the "introduction-body-summary conclusion" rule learned over and over throughout our school years does not apply to verse. When it comes to the rudest side of the artiste, however, to explain is to violate the Code of Artistic Ethics. Years back, my good poet-friend, Verlena Orr, sent me a two-inch-in-diameter lavender pin which reads in bold black letters, "FUCK ART—LET'S DANCE." I keep it in eyesight of my writing desk at all times, because, what it says to me is "don't take yourself quite *that* seriously."

However, even the self-described One-&-Only Polish-Hobo-Rodeo Poet of Flat Crick (so far) takes himself seriously enough to care about audience/reader response, the strongest of which, I'm convinced, is awarded by the freest of listeners, those aficionados who disregard—or better yet, are unaware of altogether—the factions or schools of poetry. The first time I read my free verse poems in front of an Elko audience, I was skittish. I understood then, and still understand, how hard-core cowboy poetry audiences pay staunch allegiance to, and take great pride in, the tradition. Which *means* rhyme and meter. Moreover, I'd been around enough of those squint-through-rawhide John Wayne clones who could look you square through to your brain pan and warn, "It don't rhyme, it ain't po-tree." But after years of dealing with the rank-buckin'-hoss jitters of the rodeo arena, stage fright was a mere barefooted stroll through tall-grass-snake country. And so I read, not recited (another violation), the same poems I'd read so often to college audiences. Granted, these poems had rural settings and sentiments, many of them triggered by images and emotions out of my rodeo passion. But I still expected some resistance, expected at best a verbal brawl or two at the bar in the Stockman's, and at worst, silence—the cold shoulder, cowboy style.

What a surprise—make that "honor"—for the warm, if not sometimes wild, western welcome I received instead. It made me wonder if the open country those folks lived in had something to do with the way they seemed to view the world through a wide-angle lens, while at the same time zeroing-in on the emotional honesty they respected, if not yearned for?

"Hell," I *warned* them, "these poems rhyme alright, they just rhyme more in the middle of the lines than they do out on the ends!"

"Hell," I continued, "they're like riding a bareback bronc (no halter or buck rein) — just give the poem its head and let 'er rip!"

"And if that comparison doesn't work for you," I went right for the old cowboy's marrow-of-the-soul this time, "just think of these as open range — no rhymes, *no wire!*" THEN, the sockdolager (which I've always attributed to Donald Hall who, I'd bet, could rope-and-throw the heart of most any cowpoke poetry crowd with his "Names Of Horses" poem): holding the typed page out to them, I said, "See for yourselves. It's poetry. It's jagged on the right, ain't it!" And with their robust laughter, I relaxed; I realized I'd come full circle back to the blue-collar world of my youth; somehow, that world had discovered poetry while I was away and now was proud of me for bringing more of it back to them. Every woman in that audience became my mother or sister — every man, my father or brother.

Although my first go-'round at the third annual Elko Cowboy Poetry Gathering was this grand, this revelational, I still wasn't ready to shout from the rooftops, "I've found Home!" I was teaching at the University of Montana at the time, and the pull toward that vocation was strong — though it was not then, nor has it ever been, a matter of choosing one over the other, *either* Literati *or* Lariati. If I predicted anything then, I predicted that I would participate in and contribute to both arenas until the distinctions between the two disappeared completely in my mind. I would write poetry — period — as I had always done, and let *it* fall where it may.

And then one morning at 3 a.m., after witnessing, the night before, a television segment which infuriated me and made me ashamed of the genus and species to which I belong, I roughed-out a poem titled "The Hand." As I reworked it, over the next several weeks, not once did I think of it as a cowboy poem, but my hardest and freshest critic those days was Wallace McRae, so I sent it to him first. I scribbled at the top, "Is this a cowboy poem, Wallace?"

"Hell, yes!" he printed/branded his approval in bold, deep letters. And that was all that was exchanged until months later, when the two of us sat on the main stage at Elko together in the middle of the "Montana Poets" session. The format was round robin, and it appeared that I would get an unexpected third or fourth turn at the podium. I couldn't decide on a poem, but it was late in the day and I figured that something light and funny would best fit the bill. I'd memorized a short piece by S. Omar

Barker, titled "Retired Bronc Rider." I whispered my choice to Wallace for his approval.

He whispered back, "Do 'The Hand.'"

"Not here, not now," I adamantly replied. Wallace folded his arms across his barrel chest and, in a gesture of disgust, shifted sideways in his chair to turn his back on me the best he could without being overly obvious to the audience. I read "The Hand."

The longest two-second silence of my life followed, before the crowd, a thousand or so strong, broke into sustained applause. Never before had I felt in the midst of such a large extended family, a family of friends, of kindred spirits, of partners, of soul mates, of "regular folks" who love poetry. True home is like true north — once you find it, it's hard to go wrong. It was this socio-political, anti-apartheid "Literati cowboy poem" read to a Lariati audience in, of all peculiar places, Elko, Nevada, that pointed me toward True Home:

THE HAND

In South Africa, a white aristocrat grabs
the hand of an elderly black man
sitting in the dirt on the edge
of a lush crop. The white man
picks the black man's hand up
as if it were a self-serve gasoline nozzle,
pulls it toward a reporter
and mechanically squeezes the wrist
to spread wide the thick callused fingers
and palm. The white man holds his own hand
open side-by-side. "Do you see
the difference?" he asks. "What
does his hand look like to you? How
can you say we are the same?"

"Do you see the difference?" he asks again,
the reporter stunned by what he is hearing,
while the black man sits inanimate,
his working cowboy hand
filling the camera's close-up lens
with a landscape of canyons,
coulees and arroyos, buttes and mesas, mountains

and plains the black man might have ridden,
hands shaped by pistol grip, lariat, and reins,
had he been born of another geography
and time—just another wind-burned hand
of a cavvy man, sinew and knuckle,
flesh and blood, pocked, porous, scarred,
and dark as lathered latigo. The hand
alongside the aristocrat's
tissue-paper appendage always reaching to take
even another man's hand, and own it,
and hold it open, because he knows the fist
is as big as a man's heart
and *this* is the difference he fears.

Returning to D.C. two years later to recite cowboy poetry at The Library of Congress, I was honored by a more personal response to the same poem. After our performance, a Mr. Frank Phillips thanked me for doing "The Hand." Dressed in a suit, he handed me his card embossed with the gold seal of the United States, which read "Court Systems Division—Thurgood Marshall Federal Judiciary Building." The same instant in which I wondered what it was that drew this official-looking urbanite to a cowboy poetry reading, Mr. Phillips told me—pride gleaming in his eyes—that he was Bill Pickett's great grandson. Bill Pickett. The black cowboy who "invented" bull-doggin'. Or, as my old traveling partner, Kim Zupan, once referred to him in print, "the patron saint of rodeo." I wanted to get down on one knee and kiss Frank's ring, but instead I sent him a cassette on which I recite "The Hand." In return, I received a reproduction of the 1930's movie poster, *The Bull-Dogger*, featuring a large portrait of handsome Bill Pickett.

I've recently coined for myself a simple metaphor, which sits side by side with Verlena's F.A.L.D. button in my mind's eye: CONNECT THE DOTS. As writers—hell, as human beings on planet earth—isn't that the virtue, the blessing, the grace, the gift, the skill, which delights us most? Don't we revel each time we draw a connecting line between ttwo paints, and consider it "right," and feel we're given a little better glimpse of/clue to The Big Picture? From South Africa to Augusta, Montana, to McRae's Rocker Six Cattle Company on Rosebud Crick to the main stage in Elko, Nevada, to The Library of Congress, a couple of dots seem to connect pretty wonderfully for me. And out of the five "cowboy poetry days" I spent in D.C. came another piece of writing, titled "Shoes," which attempts to break trail between a few more dots, more directly related, in part, to the slant of this essay.

But before sharing the poem "Shoes," another little side-bar seems fitting here: On Sunday morning, following the 1994 annual banquet of the Northern Plains Resource Council in Billings, at which poet Wendell Berry was the keynote speaker, Wally McRae and I and a small group of Wallace's comrades from the Council's early days were palavering in the hotel lobby. The subject of cowboy poetry arose, and before we knew it, three or four of us were round robining verses.

In the midst of our spontaneous gathering, Wendell and his wife, Tanya, on their way out to catch their flight, stopped for some quick good-byes, during which Wendell mentioned sending a cowboy poem to his good friend Donald Hall, who'd been severely ill. Donald wrote back and said that of all the beautiful get-well-soon poems he'd received, none tickled him and lifted his spirits as much as the one Wendell sent.

"I can't recall the title," Wendell said, "but it was a story about a cowboy dying and coming back as a pile of road apples." I wish now that I'd have thought quickly enough to respond, "Holy Horseshit!" But I did exclaim, with great surprise and wonderment over yet another poetic connection, "That's 'Reincarnation!' Wally wrote it!" I motioned him over to recite the poem for Wendell before the cab arrived, after which everyone parted on a joyous, jagged-on-the-right note.

I believe we are all in this snapshot called "life and poetry and death" together. I believe in art with/of distinction, but without hierarchy — because, on an even, equal plane, the thin lines between genres, disciplines, schools, cultures, etc., can be hopped across with greater pleasure and understanding by all. I don't know, or care, if my poem "Shoes" is "cowboy." I did, however, read it at the 1995 Elko Cowboy Poetry Gathering in a session (not so incidentally, a session which included Yevgeny Alexandrovich Yevtushenko, "Cossack Poet") called "Beyond the Tradition." No, not below or above, but outside, or alongside, of — or better yet, in harmony *with* the tradition.

SHOES

What atrocities befell my Slavic ancestors
during the war, I cannot say. But I've heard
Czeslaw Milosz read poems in Polish
from the pulpit of Washington D.C.'s Church
Of The Reformation. His words, at once familiar

and gorgeously foreign to my ear, were kin
to our cowboy verses lilting
through The Library of Congress
the night before. The morning after
hearing Milosz, I wept
different tears in the Holocaust Museum,
one for each mildewed shoe
heaped in a musky, dark exhibit
backdropped by large snapshots of mountains
of shoes at Auschwitz. Brogan or slipper
resting upright, did those, open to the sky,
signal to the ashes of feet
drifting from the stacks — brittle, warm
flakes of flesh finding their way
defiantly back to their shoes? I am torn for life
between the desperate need to believe
in the unfathomable, and the grimace
to forget — what I smelled, what I tasted,
what I heard and witnessed, but could not
reach out and caress. I wanted to run
my cupped hand into each shoe with hope
of finding one matched pair
still together five decades after
the condemned grandmother's, grandfather's,
husband's, wife's, sister's, brother's,
daughter's, son's cold numb fingers crawled
through their last unlacings.
                         Milosz's poems
spoke to 83 years of knowing how death
fills up a life — the suddenness of manhood and then
back to a boy reliving his fancy
for fiery workings of the village
blacksmith hammering out iron shoes
in a Lithuanian livery. Cowboy poetry, I swear,
pinged from pulpit to pews
to choir loft and cathedral ceiling

in D.C. that night. I wore sneakers out of fear
for dark city corners and hatred still
seething in the ethnocentric minds of man,
left my hat and boots in the room
and walked, bewildered in squared-off circles,
after seeing Museum and Milosz. Avoiding the faces
of everyone I passed, left me alone
in my world of shoes — leather, laces, tongues,
toes, heels, seams and eyes
of trainload upon trainload of the doomed
peeking between slats of boxcars — the coldest
exhibit you'll ever step into — where they stood
still in their shoes.

                    What I ask now is
that each of this world's soldiering poets writes life
back into one shoe of the persecuted — softly
as a mother's fingertip to her teething child's gums,
rub olive oil into the leather until you feel it
breathing again. Choose your most truthful
words, your most vital music,
worthy of being sung in synagogues, in temples,
in kivas and teepees, museums and mausoleums
and in the very church where Milosz sang,
where a woman, moved to tears
by the otherworldliness of such singing,
handed up to him a single rose — his final lines
like the gods' own chain lightning
dancing across a thousand hands
lifted in long applause. As I watched
the shaking mosaics of stained glass
windows arched above me, I feared this poem
would make its way closer to home. Now, I must
sing to you of the bugle-
beaded horse-tracks-on-buckskin
Sioux moccasin, so tiny against the black
mountains of shoes — one baby's bootee found
frozen in the snow at Wounded Knee.

Thus far, I've discovered perhaps only a couple of square feet of common ground between the Literati and the Lariati. However, from this pinnacle overlooking red-rock canyonland laid out like an eye-dazzler Navajo rug — from this vantage point — I've experienced some of the most harmonious, artistically gratifying moments in which my poetry has echoed through an audience. My wish, as is the wish of Dana Gioia (if I read him right), is to nurture this small plot, and to witness it growing until it becomes a large enough "stage" from which most any poet can speak the common language of, and to, the individuals who comprise the masses. And what we should be saying to them, again and again, is "listen while we acknowledge and pay tribute to (Y)our lives."

"RIDIN' UP THE ROCKY TRAIL FROM TOWN": PASTORAL VISION IN AMERICAN COWBOY AND RANCHING POETRY

We're the children of the open and we hate the haunts o' men,
 But we had to go to town to get the mail.
And we're ridin' home at daybreak—'cause the air is cooler then—
 All 'cept one of us that stopped behind in jail.

Shorty's nose won't bear paradin', Bill's off eye is darkly fadin',
 All our toilets show a touch of disarray,
For we found that city life is a constant round of strife
 And we ain't the breed for shyin' from a fray.

Chant your warhoop, partners dear, while the east turns pale with fear
 And the chaparral is tremblin' all aroun'
For we're wicked to the marrer; we're a midnight dream of terror
 When we're ridin' up the rocky trail from town!

—first two stanzas, Charles Badger Clark, "From Town"

Badger Clark's classic cowboy poem "From Town" opens with a telling comparison: "We're the children of the open and we hate the haunts of men." This striking contrast echoes much of the mythology that shaped the North American West, mythology in which cowboys fought "nesters" in a struggle to preserve natural innocence over urban confinement. As the poem continues, we hear the story of exuberant cowboys who embody the individual freedom identified with the frontier or the range — any region beyond the boundary of civilization. These are "buckaroos" and "bold coyotes," adept not only in the use of "leather fists," but also effective with their "leather throats." Clark's poem celebrates cowboys' night *on* the town, as well as their freedom *from* town in this comic tale. But however temporary their stay in the city, it is apparently a necessary destination, these "sons of desolation" and "outlaws of creation," still "had to go to town to get the mail . . . . " However glorious the freedom of the open range, it is in direct contact with the outposts — or "haunts" — of men.

Narratives that contrast the frontier and civilization are common in the history and literature of the North American West. In most accounts, explorers, mountain men, pioneers, forty-niners, prairie madonnas, and everyone else who followed these westering folks stamped trails and roads into broad highways; "civilization" replaced the open and the wild. Clark's children of the open were displaced by "high collared herrins'." But the eventual predominance of urban centers in the West did not preclude the continued vitality of cowboy and ranching poetry. It evolved throughout the twentieth century as a form of pastoral literature rooted in the regions where ranching continued to dominate rural economies, and cowboys still rode an open—if shrinking—range. The current renaissance of cowboy and ranching poetry, which has attracted both rural and urban audiences to cowboy poetry gatherings, demonstrates that this medium has remained a compelling form of story-telling in the United States. Much of the attraction of the poems comes from the musicality of the language and the vivid imagery typical of the tradition. Consider the next two stanzas of Clark's poem:

> We acquired our hasty temper from our friend, the centipede.
>   From the rattlesnake we learnt to guard our rights.
> We have gathered fightin' pointers from the famous bronco steed
>   And the bobcat teached us reppertee that bites.
>
> So when some high-collared herrin' jeered the garb that I was wearin'
>   'Twasn't long till we had got where talkin' ends.
> And he et his ill bred chat, with a sauce of derby hat,
>   While my merry pardners entertained his friends.
>
> *Sing 'er out, my buckaroos! let the desert hear the news.*
>   *Tell the stars the way we rubbed the haughty down*
> *We're the fiercest wolves a-prowlin' and it's just our night for howlin'*
>   *When we're riding up the rocky trail from town.*

The setting for Clark's poem is easily imagined as a turn of the century cattle drive, when the recitation of cowboy poetry began as a form of oral entertainment shared among cowboys in the 1880s and 1890s. The verse and songs that these young men created was probably shared around the campfire, in the bunkhouses, or at the saloon. Obviously a way to pass the time after a long working day in the saddle, the poems and songs that circulated also provided opportunities to recall the physical and emotional challenges of cowboy life. Traditional cowboy poetry celebrates a range of experiences, including good horses and bad cows; menacing storms and breathtaking vistas; the importance of companionship, as well as solitude with nature. Often humorous, sometimes laced with bawdy and scatological references, these poems provide a coping mechanism for a rough and unpredictable life. As the poetry evolved — sometimes taking form as cowboy songs — these bards also contributed to the evolution of pastoral literature in America.

Pastoral story-telling in general originated in North African and Mediterranean societies, such as those of the Sumerians, Hebrews, ancient Greeks and Romans. Beginning as oral bards, shepherds in these cultures communicated their values about work, nature, animal husbandry, family, and the relationship of settlement to nomadic camp.[1] Clark's brawling cow punchers are clearly descended from this line of poets, as he explains in the last stanzas of "From Town":

> Since the days that Lot and Abram split the Jordan range in halves,
> Just to fix it so their punchers wouldn't fight,
> Since old Jacob skinned his dad-in-law for six years' crop of calves
> And then hit the trail for Canaan in the night,
>
> There has been a taste for battle 'mong the men that follow cattle
> And a love of doin' things that's wild and strange,
> And the warmth of Laban's words when he missed his speckled herds
> Still is useful in the language of the range.
>
> *Sing 'er out, my bold coyotes! Leather fists and leather throats,*
> *For we wear the brand of Ishm'el like a crown.*
> *We're the sons o' desolation, we're the out-laws of creation —*
> *Ee—yow! a-ridin' up the rocky trail from town!*[2]

Significantly, it is not just the action that Clark commemorates, but the *telling* of the action: "And the warmth of Laban's words when he/missed his speckled herds/Still is useful in the language of the range." Cowboy poetry engages new generations of listeners not only because they identify with the places or labor narrated in this genre, but because the narration style or performance is infectious.

Literature that communicated pastoral ideas was eventually written by people who no longer lived on the land. Many idealized rural life and the rural past in art. Other writers and artists found the pastoral a vehicle for social commentary, particularly about the shifting relationships between the rural and urban, city and country, the developed and the wild. The long lived appeal of pastoralism can be attributed to simple-minded nostalgia, however, a pastoral sensibility offers many other possibilities. Rich in metaphor and musicality, the pastoral is versatile and powerful in its observations and commentary. And it is still practiced by women and men who live and work in the American West.[3]

These contemporary pastorialists, particularly those who are writing cowboy and ranching poetry, work within a distinctive tradition. Cowboy and ranching poets join a varied group of American writers who have offered pastoral perspectives—yeoman farmers, frontiersmen, naturalists, Native American writers, pioneers, ecologists.[4] The geographical location for the American pastoral has not been fixed, but always moving and shifting, like the riders galloping through Badger Clark's desert landscape. Cowboy poets inhabit the region where rural settlement served as a buffer between the city and "wilderness," a boundary line where much of the nation's history was determined and national mythology invented. Like other forms of pastoral literature, cowboy and ranching poetry provides a history of the contradictory experiences of the frontier as a place of both opportunity and loss, triumph and colonization, accommodation and resistance. Rather than symbolizing fixed qualities of good or evil in the west by donning the proverbial white versus black hats of western films, the cowboying poet is a liminal figure, a trickster with language who raises questions and sings songs about the ever-changing landscape he or she traverses.

Charles Badger Clark, along with Bruce Kiskaddon, Gayle Gardner, S. Omar Barker and other turn of the century cowboy poets provided some of the earliest examples of cowboy poetry. We can still hear the "language of the range" in newer versions of these trickster tales. By looking at examples of five current poets, we can see a representative range of pastoral themes that characterize cowboy poetry generally, especially the verse that is written and recited today.[5]

Early cowboys did not follow the herds as ancient nomads did; after all they were hired to work for wages in a capitalist economy. But they claimed a pastoral affinity based on the commonality of animal husbandry themes, and, like ancient pastorialists, they used vernacular language. Some contemporary poets celebrate this long lineage. Consider California cattleman and poet John C. Dofflemyer's "muses of the ranges":

> somewhere roughshod we ride in numbers small
> to cling to horses mane and slide aboard.
> our cry for life, the distant cattle call
> we come to hear the last poetic word.
> in tales we treasure all without a name
> in song we set the lonely spirit free,
> in rhyme we reach for all thet's left to tame,
> jess holdin' fast to life in poetry.
> most mounts are bred to favor easy keep
> and sweat, like folks, their worst in exercise
> and dream of barns and bales in deepest sleep
> but have new meadows blowin' in their eyes.
> we come to hold the truth thet's still survived;
> the muses of the ranges have arrived.[6]

Dofflemyer dedicated this poem to the Elko Cowboy Poetry Gathering, first organized in 1984, which attracted increased public attention to cowboy poetry. Dofflemyer explains that he traces the origins of the "distant cattle call" to ancient Greece. These new "muses" have maintained a "roughshod" existence, as a minority in "numbers small" within a larger culture that is no longer focused on the range. Dofflemyer notes the similarities between the social context in which Homeric ballads evolved and those in which cowboy poets practice their art. Both communities of poets share roots in an oral tradition that relied upon vernacular language. Dofflemyer sees Hesiod as the poet who offered "the first cries of social injustice in Europe," and Dofflemyer identifies with Hesiod's commentary on the tyrannies of town life."

A female muse of the range, Sue Wallis associates cowboy and ranching poetry with a different ancient tradition—that of Celtic history and legends. In particular, Wallis feels a kinship with the figure Brighid, "a triple warrior goddess—that is, three sisters all with the same name—one the goddess of metalworking, one the goddess of poetry and knowledge, and one the goddess of healing, especially the healing and health of herds of livestock." In "Brighid," Wallis tells a woman's story of the range, which she sees as a continuation of the kinds of rituals that might have accompanied Brighid's feast day, "which fell in the early spring time of lambing and calving," and which were "conducted in secret, performed entirely by women." In the poem, the narrator describes how the "winds of the Spring in Wyomin'" bring the story of Brighid, who was "Born neither in, nor out of a house, in the Dawn." Brighid the muse and Wallis the poet move between time and worlds, and carry the secrets of women on the range, as this stanza explains:

> In the long, dark nights just sit and listen
> To the old, old tales that a woman tells
> When no cow is in labor, no tail is switchin'.
> The best songs come in the calvin' lulls,
> When the men are sleepin'.[7]

Brighid's song comes during calving season, when these "herds women" aid in the birth of their stock. Mothers teach their daughters the ranching skills they need, as the secrets of birthing calves are passed on in this oral tradition that celebrates how labor—in all its connotations—is crucial to the health of a ranching family's enterprise.

Moreover, mothers share the mysteries of women's lives more generally, they also " . . . tell their girls / The lore of birth—the rituals and rights / Of women—and how Life hurls / Bliss and pain, joy and frights." Wallis's poem reclaims a female pastoral history, and since the life of a shepherd is obviously related to nurturing the weak and young, exploring the feminine mysteries of birthing has logically characterized many poems written by women on the land.

However, to live in close proximity to birth as a rancher is also to live with the everyday possibility of injury and death—the "pain" and "frights" of Brighid's lessons. Linda Hussa, who ranches with her husband in Cedarville, located in the Surprise Valley of northeastern California, witnesses the full range of natural forces faced by ranchers. Raising stock is hard and demanding work, at the same time as it provides sustenance. It is where a human mother comes face to face with the fierce wildness of a female coyote, for example, in Hussa's poem, "Under the Hunter Moon." The narrator, a ranch woman who has tired of "Slain lambs, guts ripped open / Magpies and blowflies / Blaating ewes with swollen bags searching the flock" heads out to meet her opponent:

> I watch her snatch mice out of the grass
>   flip them like popcorn
>   down the hatch. She is a comic

this coyote, playing, laughing
making her way steadily toward me
my fingers soft on the gold steel trigger.
Coyote stops
    looks directly at me
Her eyes hold me accountable.[8]

In Hussa's community, where sheep and cattle are still raised close to "wild nature", there are no idyllic pastures with cavorting lambs. The pastoral is sometimes interpreted as a form of "nature writing," and a poet like Hussa's direct contact with the land—and with wildlife—provides a pensive look at the relationship between human societies and the wild. Poems like Hussa's underscore the role of pastoral traditions in communicating difficult choices, and uncomfortable truths.

Hussa, like many women before her, came to ranching through marriage, and she has now lived on the edge of the Great Basin for over twenty-five years. Her poetry, grounded in the close observation of a landscape she knows intimately, often captures the deeper significance of apparently ordinary life. Attention to "dailiness" is particularly characteristic of women's writing, particularly when women were deemed responsible for a "domestic" sphere. But as Wallis's and Hussa's poems show, that sphere is not confining when family ranching demands a hand for many kinds of work. Women have always observed dramatic changes in the west, and poets like Hussa and Wallis have witnessed the difficulties that ranchers faced as economic change forced increasing numbers of family ranchers out of business and off of the land. "Cowboy poetry," Wallis writes, "is about the working cowboy, the ranching family, the folks who are out there raising beef that goes on your table, taking care of the earth they own or lease." Increasingly, she continues, they are working for "the other guy, who far too often is some faceless, nameless, mega-monster corporation." The pastoral poem has proved a powerful way to document, protest, and resist such changes.[9]

Montana poet Wallace McRae, for example, found inspiration in a pastoral tradition shaped both by participation in and separation from rural culture. McRae's family has ranched in southeastern Montana, near Forsythe, for several generations. "I think the reason I'm a rancher and do what I do is almost genetic," McRae suggests, "I was fortunate enough to be born into a ranching family that was able to hold out during the tough times of the thirties." McRae describes himself as an iconoclast among ranchers, and attributes his stance to the experiences he had away from home in college and the navy: "When I came home, I suddenly recognized the uniqueness of the culture I'd taken for granted" including its "stories, characters, taboos, land, livestock and traditions." McRae's appreciation for ranching culture intensified because he rode the modern trails between town and country, and made the difficult choice to return home to stay—unlike other rural sons and daughters of his generation who moved to town permanently.

Like others in ranching communities, McRae's appreciation for the distinctive qualities of his way of life intensified when the hungry urbanites discovered the rural resources of southeastern Montana. McRae's ranching community seemed threatened by irresponsible coal development. The North Central Power Study, a resource allocation plan, referred to southeastern Montana and northeastern Wyoming as a "national sacrifice area." McRae was outraged, like many other rural people who feel ignored by public policy makers in Washington D.C. He recalled, "So, here I am, Li'l Abner living in Dogwatch, the most unnecessary town in the U.S.A.," he remembered, "and I rebelled against this, this is ridiculous."[10]

McRae joined some of his neighbors in lobbying efforts to stop, or at least reconsider plans to develop coal. One of his most powerful poems, "Things of Intrinsic Worth," sounds a bitter alarm about the perennially destructive lure of extractive resource development in the modern West:

> Remember that sandrock on Emmells Crick
> Where Dad carved his name in 'thirteen?
> It's been blasted down into rubble
> And interred by their dragline machine.
> Where Fadhls lived, at the old Milar place,
> Where us kids stole melons at night?
> They 'dozed it up in a funeral pyre
> Then torched it. It's gone alright.
> The "C" on the hill, and the water tanks
> Are now classified "reclaimed land."
> They're thinking of building a golf course
> Out there, so I understand.
> The old Egan homestead's an ash pond
> That they say is eighty feet deep.
> The branding corral at the Douglas camp
> Is underneath a spoil heap.

And across the crick is a tipple now,
Where they load coal onto a train.
The Mae West Rock on Hay Coulee?
Just black and white snapshots remain.
There's a railroad loop and a coal storage shed
Where the bison kill site used to be.
The Guy place is gone; Ambrose's too.
Beulah Farley's a ranch refugee.

But things are booming. We've got this new school
That's envied across the whole state.
When folks up and ask, "How's things goin' down there?"
I grin like a fool and say, "Great!"
Great God, how we're doin'! We're rollin' in dough,
As they tear and they ravage the Earth.
And nobody knows . . . or nobody cares . . .
About things of intrinsic worth."[11]

This poem does not memorialize cattle drives or beloved horses, rather, it uses the memories associated with place to register frustration and anger at industrial progress. It remembers settled ranchers that have seen the places that preserved memories and community—"Egan's homestead" or the "Mae West Rock on Hay Coulee"—destroyed, "blasted down into rubble." The poet evokes the first humans in what would become Montana, who were displaced by change—Native Americans who used the "bison kill site." Once coal mining reduced the landscape and its stories to "rubble," one must rely on the poet's memories to find connection to the past.

Unwanted change may originate in the city, and the contemporary cowboy can no longer dodge every encounter like those imagined by Badger Clark. Like McRae, both John Dofflemyer and Sue Wallis developed a sense of needing to defend rural culture after they had left family ranches for school. Traveling south to attend the Webb School in Claremont, California, Dofflemyer experienced the alienation of being different from urbane, cosmopolitan preppies. But the city provided more than a negative goad. He recalls that his inspiration to write poetry came in response to both his sense of being from a "rigid", rural background that was challenged by new influences in the city, particularly the political turmoil of the Viet Nam War, and his desire to affirm admirable aspects of his rural upbringing. His exposure to poets in classes and book-stores around Los Angeles led him to models like "Shakespeare, Gary Snyder, Robert Creeley."[12]

Dofflemyer's art, like that of so many cowboy and ranching poets, results from his struggles with multiple influences. For example, Dofflemyer's upbringing taught him that "there was a fine line between a good story teller and a windbag," which may have shaped his resistance to some of the narrative tradition that dominates classic cowboy poetry. He has early memories of "escaping from his playpen" to go off to the fields to listen to "Okies" share tales—often in competitive story-telling sessions. "They could tell some stories", he recalled, "You know whether you've got a story to match theirs or not—a child or young man could try to match them, but there's no way, he doesn't have the experience, either in story-telling or in life." As Dofflemyer grew older, he shared stories with the men he worked with, "They're not necessarily off-color or sexual but ones men would appreciate, and they're true stories, they're about half crazy, symbolism, humorous—funny. But I don't do them in my poems—the only stories I'd put down in my poetry are obviously, outrageously, not true, there's no pretense of being true."[13] Multiple oral traditions shaped Dofflemyer's craft, but he was simultaneously influenced by the poets he found in his education and in urban bookstores.

Whereas ranch sons and daughters like Wallis, Dofflemyer and McRae left their homes for the education of urban campuses and then returned home to reconsider the values of rural life, Montana poet Paul Zarzyski represents a different road taken by many contemporary cowboy poets. Zarzyski left home after college in Wisconsin to follow a "rodeo road" into the rural West. Zarzyski wanted to study poetry with the distinguished poet Richard Hugo, then teaching at the University of Montana. Zarzyski's choice was partially inspired by Hugo's poem "Driving Montana," which ends with the lines " . . . You are lost / in miles of land without people, without / one fear of being found, in the dash / of rabbits, soar of antelope, swirl / merge and clatter of streams."[14] Zarzyski's own migration forms a basis for the lyrical pastoral poem, "Luck of the Draw," where a young boy, lured by the cowboy heroes he saw on television (most definitely a gift from town), anticipates the beauty and magic of the West. Consider the first stanza of "The Luck of the Draw":

> That holy moment I rode the bay,
> Whispering Hope, this rodeo arena—
> like a shrine I return to, like a sanctuary
> or religion itself—was filled with bawling holler,

dust and hoofbeats. The blur of cowboy colors
shimmered brilliant as boyhood Septembers
among birch and sugar maples, where I played
decked-out like TV bronc twister,
Stoney Burke.

In stanza two, Zarzyski's poem continues with other memories of the sheer joy of adolescent physical freedom — a freedom that would eventually become synonymous with Horace Greeley's West, the west of promise for young men.

But that was before
high school fans cheered us
galloping against rivals under gladiator lights
those fall Fridays in the pits, number 72
afire for 48 minutes of forearm shiver
and crack-back block.
It's hard to believe
there was a time I forgot the roughstock
rider gutting it out
to the final gun, the whole
gridiron game's-worth of physical grit
concentrated, pressed into one play,
into one 8-second ride. All I needed was a horse
and the words of Horace Greeley in a dream,
a western pen pal, a cowboy
serial flashback, some sign or cue
to make me imagine the chutegate
thrown open to the snap — cleats
and spurs, chaps and pads, high kicks,
hard hits and heartbeats synchronized
a thousand miles apart.

Zarzyski merged his twin passions in the West — rodeo and poetry — and became one of the most innovative of contemporary cowboy poets. He embraced rodeo with a conscious awareness that he came to the arena late, after the prime of male adolescence and the prime of the "open country" west. Thus his poem conveys the pastoral poet's longing for the place and time that has just slipped away, and must be recreated in art. Listen to the closing stanzas:

I left home barely
soon enough to make one good
bucking horse ride
across a vast canvas of Russell landscape
backdropped by Heart Butte under a fuchsia sky
in Cascade, Montana.
                    Through these cottonwoods,
high above the Missouri River's silent swirls,
the flicking together of leaves
is the applause of small green hands, children
thrilled by a winning ride, by their wildest wish
beginning, as everything begins, with luck
of the draw, with a breeze in the heat,
with whispering hope — a first breath
blessed by myth, or birth, in the West.[15]

Migration is a spiritual and geographical pilgrimage in "Luck of the Draw," and the poet's meditation recalls loss and renewal, childhood fantasies and small town football glory — experiences intensified in the rodeo arena. Zarzyski's West remains a place where even greenhorns — with no roots of blood ties to the region — can travel a road akin to that of Badger Clark's wild rangers, come late to their dreams, and prove their cowboy worth.

Zarzyski found in poetry and rough stock riding an opportunity to "buck the American Dream hoax" that he felt had hemmed in his parent's life in hometown Hurley, Wisconsin. But going west to buck and rhyme also enabled Zarzyski to come "full circle," back to that world. He explores those connections in the poetry collection, *Blue Collar Light*.[16] In that introduction, Zarzyski attributes his love for words — *his* famous "repartee that bites" — to inspiration born from the Hurley blue collar oral culture. The immigrant background of his family and neighbors exposed him to a diversity of language. The Hurley phone book listed names like Studs Morghetti, Ham Cavosie, Urho Tuominen, Italo Bensoni . . . . Zarzyski points out that these names formed a "very significant collection of poetry." Discovering cowboy poetry — especially the power of oral recitation provided by the classics — connected Zarzyski with his heritage. In towns like Butte, Montana, he also discovered a rodeo partner with the same "musical" ethnic background, a connection to which he pays tribute in the poem "Why I Like Butte, or How's She Goin' Today, Just?"[17]

Zarzyski learned to recite cowboy classics, and then adapt his original poems to the meters of that poetry. He loved the community that gathered at Elko, Nevada, because it was primarily made up of audiences that wanted to hear, as Zarzyski calls it, "the ring and ricochet of lingo off the stirrup bone of the middle ear." Reciting at gatherings meant that Zarzyski was saying poems to "people like those I grew up with, and they did not have to decode them. I was able to come full circle from the gridiron and the woods and trout streams . . . ."[18] Zarzyski's migration west was not one-directional. Like other poets described here, his poetry evolved as he explored the pastoral borderland between east and west, country and city, past and present.

Cowboy labor helped build the West at the turn of the century, and Cowboy imagination shaped the imaginary West through poetry and song. Ironically, they began to make these contributions at the same time that they became figures in the nation's frontier mythology. Recent histories of the American West challenge the accuracy of presenting westward expansion as a process in which lone individuals like mountain men, cowboys and pioneers could behave like "children of the open."[19] The territory "opened"—that is, made available to people for hunting, grazing, mining, timber, and agricultural development, had previously supported Native Americans, of course. American Indians gave up land in unfair treaties, or were forced or tricked by the United States government to relinquish territory and hunting rights. American Indian land was then claimed by EuroAmericans pushing west. When cowboy poetry was first recited around campfires on the plains, Lakota and Comanche bands still hunted there. Autobiographies from early cowboys like Teddy Blue Abbott and Andy Adams attest to fights with Indians, but also to the increasingly desperate plight of these "enemies."

Nevertheless, in this short lived era of cattle boom and bust, the young men who went up the trail experienced an exhilarating measure of freedom on the open range, which they documented in story and song. Cowboy poetry, and the ranching literature that followed it, documents the desire for a separation from town, but at the same time, the limitations of open space and the inevitable taming of wild nature and natures. In the same era when conservationists sounded the alarm about preserving America's undeveloped wilderness, cowboys experienced wild places on a daily basis, and wrote about those places in their verse. Badger Clark's cowboys may have learned some lessons from the Bible, but also from nature itself as they adopted the temperament of "centipede, rattlesnake, bronco, and bobcat." The "rocky trail from town," apparently offers no easy passage, and it takes these cowboys back to a wild, uncivilized range, unspoiled by the creep of progress and civilization. They remain the "sons o' desolation," "outlaws of creation." If as some historians observe, late nineteenth century Americans craved the call of the wild, the cowboy was their beacon.

Contemporary cowboy and ranching poets share Clark's suspicion about town, especially since the city became particularly large, impersonal, a center for bureaucratic management of western lands—including "national sacrifice areas." Mindful of the need to communicate with urban America and wanting to challenge negative cultural assumptions about ranching and rural America, poets battle the city slicker with words not fists. Some even seek common ground with urbanites, especially those intrigued with the pastoral sentiments in cowboy and ranching poetry. Cowboy poetry continues to negotiate the complex pastoral legacy of westering peoples.

NOTES

[1] There is an extensive body of materials on the ancient pastoral. I found David Halperin, *Before Pastoral: Theocritus and the Ancient Tradition of Bucolic Poetry* (New Haven, Connecticut: Yale University Press, 1983), especially helpful.

[2] Charles Badger Clark Jr., in *Sun and Saddle Leather: A Collection of Poems* (Tucson, Arizona: Westerners International, 1915), pp. 38-40.

[3] Recent scholars have celebrated and debated the importance of "place" in Western regional literature. Taking their inspiration from leading practitioners like Wallace Stegner, critics evaluate the relevance of geographical location for western writers, especially those who are sensitive to economic and environmental change. Pastoral literature has often addressed such changes, and cowboy and ranching poetry are examples of the kind of "revised pastoral" advocated by critics like Glen Love, in his essay "Revaluing Nature: Toward an Ecology Criticism" in *Western American Literature* (November 1990): 201-215. The folk art status of cowboy poetry has meant that it is rarely considered in discussions of either the American pastoral or regional literature, yet cowboy and ranching poets take up many of the creative and ideological themes signaled by both "pastoral" and "regional" literature.

[4] On the pastoral in American literature, see Leo Marx, "Pastoralism in America," in *Ideology and Classic American Literature*, ed. Sacvan Berkovich and Myra Jehlen (London: Cambridge University Press, 1986), pp. 36-69.

[5] Beginning in 1993, I have interviewed selected cowboy and ranching poets who were willing to share their autobiographical stories with me. Some of these interviews are noted in this essay.

[6] John C. Dofflemyer, *"muses of the ranges"* (Lemon Cove, California: Dry Crik Press, 1991), pp. 12-15.

[7] Poem and commentary in Sue Wallis, *Another Green Grass Lover: Selected Poetry of Sue Wallis* (Lemon Cove, California: Dry Crik Press, 1994), p. 24.

[8] Linda Hussa, *Where the Wind Lives: Poems from the Great Basin* (Salt Lake City, Utah: Gibbs-Smith Publisher, 1994), p. 48.

[9] Sue Wallis, "Throw Back the Gates: Contemporary Cowboy Poetry," *Dry Crik Review* (Summer 1992): p. 17. Interviews with Sue Wallis, 3-24-94, and Linda Hussa, 8-96.

[10] Interview with Wallace McRae, 8-18-94.

[11] Wallace McRae, *Cowboy Curmudgeon and Other Poems* (Salt Lake City, Utah: Gibbs-Smith Publisher, 1992), p. 131.

[12] Interview with John C. Dofflemyer, 10-10-93.

[13] Interview with John C. Dofflemyer, 10-10-93.

[14] Richard Hugo, *Making Certain It Goes On: The Collected Poems of Richard Hugo* (New York, New York, W.W. Norton and Co., 1984), p. 204.

[15] "The Luck of the Draw" can be found in Paul Zarzyski's *All This Way for the Short Ride: Roughstock Sonnets, 1971-1996* (Sante Fe, New Mexico: Museum of New Mexico Press, 1996), p. 27.

[16] Paul Zarzyski, "Take Home Pay," in *Blue-Collar Light: Poems by Paul Zarzyski* (West Sacramento, California: Red Wing Press, 1998), pp. 3-13.

[17] "Why I Like Butte or: How's She Goin' Today, Just?" in *I am Not a Cowboy* (Lemon Cove, California, Dry Crik Press, 1995), p. 14. Interview with Paul Zarzyski, 10-12-93.

[18] Interview with Paul Zarzyski, 10-12-93.

[19] See for example, Patricia Nelson Limerick, *The Legacy of Conquest: The Unbroken Past of the American West* (New York, New York: W.W. Norton and Co...., 1987).

J. B. Allen, a life-long cowboy, began writing poetry in his fiftieth year. In his introduction to Allen's *The Medicine Keepers* (Grey Horse Press — book and CD), the late, great Buck Ramsey described the impulse that turned the wrangler to verse, and its consequences: "Something deep within him and out of a past beyond memory took hold of him and, without wishing or willing it, he was possessed of an eloquence in the tribal lingo and a dead-on-ear for the rhythms of traditional verse that caused poem after poem to flow from him in finished language." Now a county commissioner in Whiteface, Texas, Allen still works cattle for outfits a day's driving distance from his current home.

Virginia Bennett, with her husband, Pe¡te, manages the Tice Ranch in Twisp, Washington. Her books include *Canyon of the Forgotten* (1998), *Legacy of the Land* (1993, 1995), *Storms on the Divide* (1991), and *Rode Hard and Put Away Wet* (1990). Her poetry has appeared in numerous anthologies, and she has recorded and performed her verse on videos, radio, and television. She appears regularly at many festivals, including the national Cowboy Poetry Gathering in Elko, Nevada. She is also an innovative author of Cowboy poetry for children. Writing about Virginia Bennett's poetry, Sir Christopher Ball, Chancellor of the University of Derby in Oxford, England, makes the point that it "celebrates the traditions and reality of the American West. She has a fresh eye and distinctive voice that confirm her standing as a true poet."

Robert R. Brown, born and raised in California's Central Valley, grew up in a migratory family of farm and ranch laborers. After serving four years in the United States Air Force during the Korean War, Brown served for thirty-one years with the California Highway Patrol. In retirement, he focuses on poetry and stories, and has recently completed a western novel.

Born in Edinburgh, Scotland, in 1954, raised in suburbs and on Air Force bases around the world, **Laurie Wagner Buyer** came West in 1975 and moved high in the Montana backcountry. Since 1988, she and her husband, Mick, a fourth generation rancher, have lived on the South Fork of the South Platte River near Fairplay, Colorado. Buyer attended George Williams College, and graduated from Montana State University with highest honors. Her three volumes of poetry include *Glass-eyed Paint in the Rain* (High Plains Press, 1996), *Braintanning Buckskin* (Dry Crik Press, 1996), and *Blue Heron* (Dry Crik Press, 1995). Her poems have appeared in numerous anthologies and magazines, and her non-fiction articles and photographs appear in both regional and national newspapers and magazines.

John C. Dofflemyer lives and works in Lemon Cove, California. An influential editor and essayist as well as a poet, he edited *Dry Crik Review*, and the highly regarded anthology, *Maverick Western Verse* for Gibbs-Smith, Publisher.

Dana Gioia, whose Mexican grandfather and great-grandfather worked as cowboys, is the author of two books of poetry, *Daily Horoscope* and *The Gods of Winter,* and the essay collection, *Can Poetry Matter?*. The title essay, reprinted here, originally appeared in *The Atlantic Monthly*, provoking more reader response than¡ any article published there in decades. Gioia is also the editor of several bestselling literary anthologies, and his poems appear in the Norton Anthology of Poetry. He has recently completed an opera libretto, *Nosferatu, for the composer Alva Henderson.*

Tami Haaland, a recent graduate of the Bennington College M.F.A. Program, lives and teaches in Billings, Montana, where she has just designed an online composition course. A descendant of Montana homesteaders, her poems have appeared in a number of magazines.

Donald Hall is the author of twelve volumes of verse, including *Kicking the Leaves, The One Day,* and *The Museum of Clear Ideas*, memorable books for children, and many books of prose (including *String Too Short to Be Saved, Their Ancient Glittering Eyes: Remembering Poets and More Poets,* and *Seasons at Eagle Pond.*) A former Poet Laureate of New Hampshire (where he lives on the family's ancestral farm), Hall's many awards include the National Book Critics Circle Award, the *Los Angeles Times* Book Prize, and the Caldecott Medal.

Linda M. Hasselstrom, born in Texas in 1943, lived on a South Dakota ranch from 1947 to 1992. She now accepts applications from women writers who want to work with her on their own writing during the summer at her ranch home, Windbreak House. Hasselstrom has, for the last thirty years, made her living by ranch work, freelance writing and workshops in writing and publishing. A journal of the spring following her husband's death appeared in LIFE magazine in July, 1989, when she was named Author of the Year to the South Dakota Hall of Fame, and received the Governor's Award for Distinction in Creative Achievement. With Nancy Curtis and Gayell Collier, she edited the anthology *Leaning into the Wind: Women Write from the Heart of the West* (Houghton Mifflin, 1997), and wrote its introduction.

Linda Hussa is a poet, writer, and rancher living with her husband, John, on their ranch in Surprise Valley, California. Her poems appear in numerous reviews and anthologies such as *Graining the Mare, Maverick Western Verse,* and *Between Earth and Sky: Cowboy Poets of the New West.* Her books of poetry are *Where the Wind Lives* (Gibbs-Smith Publisher, 1994), and *Ride the Silence* (The Black Rock Press, 1995). Hussa is also the author of *Diary of a Cow Camp Cook* (non-fiction), and a biography published by the University of Oklahoma Press, *Lige Langston: Sweet Iron* (1999). Hussa was the recipient of Nevada's 1999 Silver Pen Award.

Tony Johnston, a native Californian and a graduate of Stanford University, spent much of her childhood on her grandfather's ranch in Paso Robles. Primarily an author for young people, she has published over one hundred books, including five volumes of poetry, most recently *An Old Shell: Poems of the Galápagos* (Farrar, Straus & Giroux, 1999). In 1979, "The Wagon," a story poem, received the Simon Wiesenthal Center Award for children's tolerance literature.

Maxine Kumin has received the Pulitzer Prize, the Poets' Prize, the Levinson Prize, and the Ruth Lilly Prize for her poetry. The author of twelve books of poetry, four novels, a collection of short stories, three books of essays, and a number of books for children, she lives and writes in New Hampshire.

Linda McCarriston is on sabbatical from the University of Alaska, Anchorage, and living in Big Horn, Wyoming, with her mare, Moriah, two dogs and a cat. "Most days," she writes, "my ten-year-old neighbor, Sara, and I ride among the Texas longhorns on her daddy's ranch." Her third book of poetry, *Little River,* is forthcoming from Jessie Lendennie's Salmon Press of Knockeven, Cliffs of Moher, Ireland.

Nancy McLelland teaches in the English Department at Mendocino College in Ukiah, California. Inspired by wide reading and her many visits to the Cowboy Poetry Gathering in Elko, Nevada, her essay here speaks to the heart of this anthology's highest aspirations.

Wallace McRae's poems have appeared in numerous anthologies and publications. For years he has recited his poems on radio and television, and has performed at the National Cowboy Hall of Fame. He is often a featured performer at the annual Cowboy Poetry Gathering in Elko, Nevada. In 1990, he became the first Cowboy poet to receive a National Heritage Award from the National Endowment for the Arts. With his family, McRae manages a 30,000-acre cow-calf ranch in Forsyth, Montana.

Joel Nelson ranches with his family in Texas. A veteran of Vietnam, he has performed his poetry at festivals and gatherings throughout the country. His work is included in the important anthology, *New Cowboy Poetry: A Contemporary Gathering*. He has said that his poetry reflects "the appreciation I have for the modern cowboy and his absolute refusal to turn loose of what was good from the past."

Kathy Ogren directs the Johnston Center for Integrative Studies at the University of Redlands in California. She has interviewed and written about many of the contributors to this volume, and recently taught a class in which she juxtaposed Hesiod and Cowboy poetry as versions of the pastoral. Her essay here was specifically written for this collection.

Thelma Poirier ranches with her husband near Fir Mountain in the deep southern Saskatchewan. Her books of poetry include *Double Visions* and *Grasslands*, the latter based on her presentation to the public hearing for the formation of the Grasslands National Park in Canada. Other published work includes a book for children, *The Bead Pot*. In 1978, she edited the anthology *Cowgirls: 100 Years of Writing the Range*. A widely anthologized poet and performer at festivals throughout the West, she helped organize the Canadian Cowboy Festival in Calgary.

The late **Buck Ramsey** spent many years working on the big ranches along the Canadian River in the Texas Panhandle. One of the most influential and revered contemporary poets of the West, Ramsey recited his poems and sang traditional old cowboy songs at festivals and gatherings throughout the country.

Liam Rector's two volumes of poetry are *The Sorrow of Architecture* (Dragon Gate, 1984) and *American Prodigal* (Story Line Press, 1994). The author of an anthology of criticism, *The Day I Was Older: On the Poetry of Donald Hall* (Story Line Press, 1989). A graduate of the Writing Seminars at Johns Hopkins and the Kennedy School of Government at Harvard, he has received fellowships in poetry from the Gugenheim Foundation and the National Endowment for the Arts. He has administered literary programs at the Folger Shakespeare Library, the Academy of American Poets, and Associated Writing Programs, and is currently executive director of the Writing Seminars at Bennington College in Vermont.

A poet, song writer, singer, and playwright whose particular interest is the history and peoples of the Great Plains, **Andy Wilkinson** has recorded four albums of original music and has written two plays, "Charlie Goodnight's Last Night," performed by Barry Corbin, and the musical drama, "My Cowboy's Gift." His work has received several awards, including the Texas Historical Foundation's John Ben Sheppered, Jr. Craftsmanship Award, and three National Western Heritage "Wrangler" Awards, two for original music and one for poetry. In addition to his writing, he tours extensively in a variety of venues in the U.S. and abroad. He lives in Lubbock, Texas.

Paul Zarzyski, of Montana, is a former bareback rider. He has performed his work at the Elko Cowboy Poetry Gathering, The Library of Congress, Festival Hall in London, the Pro Rodeo Hall of Fame, The Stockman's Hall of Fame in Australia, and elsewhere. His seven books and chapbooks include *All This Way for the Short Ride; Roughstock Sonnets 1971-1996* (Museum of New Mexico Press, 1996), which won the Western Heritage Award from the National Cowboy Hall of Fame in Oklahoma City, and *Blue-Collar Light* (Red Wing Press, 1998).

COWBOY POETRY ANTHOLOGIES OF NOTE

LEANING INTO THE WIND:
WOMEN WRITE FROM THE HEART OF THE WEST
    HOUGHTON MIFFLIN, 1997

HOME ON THE RANGE
    DIAL BOOKS, 1997

SOMETHING THAT A COWBOY KNOWS
    GIBBS-SMITH, 1996

HUMOROUS COWBOY POETRY
    GIBBS-SMITH, 1996

GRAINING THE MARE: THE POETRY OF RANCH WOMEN
    GIBBS-SMITH, 1995

MAVERICK WESTERN VERSE
    GIBBS-SMITH, 1994

COWBOY LOVE POETRY: VERSE FROM THE HEART OF THE WEST
    ANGEL CITY PRESS, 1994

THE COWGIRL COMPANION
    HYPERION, 1993

NEW COWBOY POETRY: A CONTEMPORARY GATHERING
    GIBBS-SMITH, 1990

COWBOY POETRY: A GATHERING
    GIBBS-SMITH, 1985